The Economics of Higher Education

The Economics of Higher Education

An Analysis of Taxes versus Fees

John Creedy

The Truby Williams Professor of Economics
University of Melbourne, Australia

Edward Elgar

Published by
Edward Elgar Publishing Limited
Gower House
Croft Road
Aldershot
Hants GU11 3HR
England

Edward Elgar Publishing Company
Old Post Road
Brookfield
Vermont 05036
USA

British Library Cataloguing in Publication Data

Creedy, John
  Economics of Higher Education:Analysis
  of Taxes Versus Fees
  I. Title
  379.118

Library of Congress Cataloguing in Publication Data

Creedy, John, 1949–
    The economics of higher education : an analysis of taxes versus
fees / John Creedy.
        p.   cm.
    Includes bibliographical references and index.
    1. Education, Higher–Finance.   2. Education, Higher–Economic
aspects.   I. Title.
LB2341.98.C74   1995
379.1'18–dc20

94-21288
CIP

ISBN 1 85278 935 2

Printed in Great Britain by
Hartnolls Ltd, Bodmin, Cornwall

Contents

Figures

Tables

Acknowledgements

This book is based largely on work which was originally carried out jointly with Patrick Francois, as shown by the joint papers listed in the bibliography. In recent years Patrick has been studying for a doctorate at the University of British Columbia, Canada, so has been unable to participate in the production of this book. He should therefore not be held responsible for any of its shortcomings. The original material has been extensively reorganized, rewritten and augmented, and I am grateful to the Editors of the journals for permission to use the material here.

This kind of project involves a huge amount of typing and re-typing, and I have been fortunate in benefiting from wordprocessing by Julie Carter, who dealt with the major burden, along with Margaret Lochran and Sally Nolan. Their splendid work is very much appreciated.

I have presented various parts of the book in seminars at Curtin University in Western Australia; the Universities of Nottingham and Reading, and the Institute of Fiscal Studies, in England; and the Pennsylvania State University in the United States. I am very grateful to the seminar participants for comments and suggestions. I should also like to thank the members of the Economics Department at Penn State for their hospitality during a visit when work was carried out on the later stages of this book.

The work was supported by two Australian Research Council grants, for which I am very grateful indeed.

Preface

There has been a great deal of debate about the appropriate method of financing higher education. For example, to what extent should higher education be financed from taxation or from fees? What are the implications of collecting fees later in life through the use of a tax surcharge? What are the redistributive implications of tax-financed higher education grants?

It is argued that much of the debate has ignored some of the important interdependencies involved. Although it is recognized that possible external effects of higher education are important, the precise way in which these affect the decision regarding taxes versus fees is seldom modelled. The role of the government's budget constraint is also seldom examined explicitly, so that analyses are typically very partial. For example, the use of higher subsidies means that tax rates must be higher, as the need for government revenue is greater, and this can have incentive and other effects.

An associated point is that the role of 'deferred fees' is seldom considered fully; that is, as higher grants are given to those who invest in higher education, taxes must be raised, but this means that those who receive the grants pay higher taxes over the remainder of their working lives. The deferred fee element is larger the higher is the progressivity of the income tax system. In the large literature on the 'rate of return' to higher education, estimates are typically based on average age–earnings profiles from cross-sectional data. However, given a dispersion of abilities in the population, there is a distribution of rates of return and, in a general equilibrium context, the rate of return at the margin (where it is just worthwhile investing in higher education) will always be equal to the real rate of interest. Even the arithmetic mean rate of return may provide misleading information about educational choices when the tax system is changed simultaneously.

A further aspect that requires more serious attention than is given in popular debates is the way in which the government's decision is modelled. The subject of financing higher education is an example of the 'dual decision' aspect in public economics. Thus, individuals make decisions given their objectives (usually modelled as maximizing utility), subject to constraints which include variables, such as tax rates, which are set by the government. At the same time the government must make decisions about tax rates which achieve its objective, subject to its budget constraint, the satisfaction of which depends in turn on the endogenous decisions taken by individuals. The government may be considered either as choosing those tax rates which it believes are supported by a majority of the voters, or it may be modelled as maximizing some social welfare function, which will typically involve some explicit trade-off between equity and efficiency.

This book examines these issues within the context of a fully specified model which is capable of handling the many interdependencies involved. The model allows for dispersion of abilities, the individual's decision to invest in higher education, the government's choice of higher education grant, along with the government's budget constraint. Alternative assumptions about the external effects of higher education are introduced into the model. The model is used to examine the effects of alternative tax and grant systems on the distribution of lifetime income within a cohort of individuals, and is extended to allow for the general equilibrium effects of other social transfers to the low-paid and the use of means-testing of grants. The special problems arising from majority voting over progressive income taxation in a multi-period framework are also examined in detail.

The analysis inevitably involves a certain amount of technical material, in view of the fact that qualitative economic analysis of these issues is rather limited. However, the introductory chapter attempts to provide a non-technical discussion of the framework of analysis and the results. The interested reader may not wish to read all the chapters in the order in which they are presented, but will find that Chapter 1 gives a relatively quick insight into the nature of the book.

1.   Introduction and outline

In the course of a review of a book consisting of 88 papers that give a 'genuine overview of the economics of education', Blaug, himself a leading authority on the subject, lamented that 'the economics of education now lies dead in the mind of both professional economists and professional educators' (1989, p. 331). In adapting, perhaps subconsciously, a comment made by Walter Bagehot over a hundred years ago about the state of political economy in general, that 'it lies rather dead in the public mind', it would also have been appropriate to use Bagehot's following statement that, 'Not only does it not excite the same interest as formerly, but there is not exactly the same confidence in it' (1885, p. 4). A major reason given by Blaug for the 'theoretical and empirical stagnation' which he observed in the economics of education is that there is still not a satisfactory answer to the question of whether it is cognitive knowledge or behavioural traits which make educated workers valuable to employers. Furthermore, 'we cannot specify, much less measure, the externalities generated by educated individuals' (1989, p. 332).

Faced with this kind of authoritative judgement, any new book on the subject must be presented with a considerable amount of diffidence. This is certainly the case with the present volume, which does not even attempt to explore the fundamental issues or to provide empirical estimates of elusive concepts mentioned by Blaug. The present study is perhaps best described as being concerned with some of the welfare and public finance aspects of higher education. In this context it is relevant to refer to the further criticism by Blaug of the book under review, that 'the application of standard welfare economics applied to education is never given its proper due' (1989, p. 334). Indeed, Blaug was critical of the tendency of many authors to list the various types of external benefit and then infer with confidence that there is a strong case for substantial state subsidies. The widespread use of this kind of argument has also been noted in the survey by Hope and Miller (1988), and it is to be found in numerous text books.

The present volume considers the use of fees versus taxation for the finance of higher education in a framework that pays special attention to some of the interdependencies involved. In particular, the use of subsidies, in the form of a higher education grant to students, involves, via the

1

government's budget constraint, an increase in taxation. This increase in income taxation imposes an obvious burden on those who do not invest in higher education, but it is not a 'free' good from the point of view of the grant recipients who must pay higher taxes than otherwise during their working lives. Such higher taxes impose what may be called a deferred fee.

Even if it can be shown that there is a substantial external effect resulting from the higher education of a minority of the population, such that all people benefit, the appropriate policy response depends on the relevant *marginal* benefits and costs. It is thus important to consider not just the distribution of those marginal costs and benefits but also the decision-taking mechanism of the government. The present book uses both a public choice framework, involving majority voting over the level of a grant, and a now-standard welfare economics approach which involves the maximization of a social welfare function. In view of the fact that some people are likely to be made worse off while others are better off, the analysis cannot be restricted to Pareto improvements and the implications of explicit distributional judgements have to be considered.

In focusing on these public finance interdependencies, it is necessary to construct a highly simplified model. A certain amount of technical analysis of the model is therefore required in order to obtain a clear understanding of the nature of the interdependencies. The purpose of the present chapter is however to attempt to describe the main features of the analysis and its context in a non-technical manner. The analysis inevitably ignores many aspects of the finance of higher education which are important, in order to focus on a narrower range of issues which seem to have been given relatively less attention in the literature.

Section 1.1 briefly discusses some of the standard arguments for subsidizing higher education and outlines the interdependencies examined later. The basic framework of analysis used is presented in section 1.2, involving individuals' investment decisions, the government's budget constraint and an equilibrium in which all plans are mutually consistent. Section 1.3 examines the majority voting equilibrium of the model and considers its comparative static properties. The use of a social welfare function defined in terms of the net lifetime incomes of individuals is considered in section 1.4. Finally, section 1.5 provides a very brief outline of subsequent chapters.

1.1   SUBSIDIES FOR HIGHER EDUCATION

In most industrialized countries there are substantial public subsidies, financed by general taxation, for higher education. Even in the United States, which has many private universities, there is a great deal of public support for the large 'Land Grant' universities. In Britain and Australia, for example, there is only one private university in each country, and extensive student grant systems exist. Large subsidies exist despite the fact that higher education does not have all the characteristics of standard 'public goods'. In particular, its provision is subject to excludability and rivalry. Nevertheless, several other rationales are usually given for tax-financed subsidies. First, it is argued that higher education is subject to market failure because it is essentially an investment good involving a long time horizon and consequently uncertain returns, combined with the imperfection of capital markets. The prospect of uncertain future higher earnings does not provide collateral for a loan. The high costs, involving forgone earnings as well as direct costs in the form of fees, are consequently often met by intra-family (inter-generational) transfers. This may be thought to perpetuate wealth inequalities and reduce social mobility. For further discussion see Hare and Ulph (1982).

A second reason given for the view that higher education will not be consumed at the socially optimal level without some form of subsidy is that it is a 'merit good'. This argument is of course essentially paternalistic, with the government taking the view that it knows 'better' than individuals what is good for them (as with the prohibition of certain goods). There is little doubt that this kind of argument provides part of the rationale for primary and secondary education being compulsory in many countries, but it is less convincing in the case of higher education. Not surprisingly, the merit good argument is fairly controversial; for example, Becker (1974) has argued that its application can in some circumstances actually reduce the consumption of higher education. For further discussion of the merit good argument in this context, see Arcelus and Levine (1986).

Third, a widely cited reason for tax-financed support is that higher education generates positive externalities which contribute to the general growth of the economy. For example, it involves an investment in human capital which yields a flow of returns over the working life to the investing individuals, but there are additional benefits which cannot be appropriated by those individuals. This argument is also controversial. On the one hand there is a very large 'growth accounting' literature which has attempted to quantify the contribution of higher education to economic growth and generally supports the view that such externalities are significant. A long list of external benefits have been suggested in the literature, including the suggestion that individuals gain utility from the knowledge that other people have received higher education; see Blaug (1970) for a discussion of many potential benefits. On the other hand, some people have argued that external benefits are negligible. In reviewing the literature, Hope and Miller (1988, p. 40) suggest that, 'whilst a sceptical attitude towards the externalities associated with higher education is appropriate, the fact that they have largely defied measurement (by both protagonists and antagonists) suggests one should refrain from being dogmatic'.

The present book actually ignores non-pecuniary and consumption-related external effects. Emphasis is instead placed on a type of externality which can arise from interdependencies, in the production process, between skilled and unskilled individuals. This means that the existence of a larger proportion of skilled workers raises the productivity of *all* workers. This sort of argument has been modelled formally in an important paper by Johnson (1984), but is implicit in some of the large literature on growth accounting. The debate is sometimes confused by a desire to regard the additional tax revenue, arising from the higher earnings generated by higher education, as a form of external effect. It seems best, however, to make a clear distinction between this effect which arises from a change in the tax base and those interdependencies in the production process mentioned above.

A further argument for the use of tax-financed subsidies involves the value judgement in favour of income redistribution. Given that the tax and transfer system generally involves 'second-best' policies, and cannot always achieve distributional objectives, it is argued that direct subsidies can have a valuable redistributive role. A somewhat different approach is that of Lommerud (1989) who uses a model in which individuals' utility depends on their relative position in the income distribution and suggests that 'it might be optimal to tax away some of the differences in people's labour income – and to use educational subsidies to restore people's incentives to undertake education' (1989, p. 651). In the present context, however, the typical argument in favour of subsidies as a way to increase equality cannot really be applied, given a strong correlation between income earning ability and the ability to benefit from higher education. As suggested by Hope and Miller (1988, p. 42) in the Australian context, 'The abolition of tuition charges in 1974, which provided an across-the-board subsidy to all students at the tax payer's expense, may thus be viewed as a redistribution from the poor(er) to the rich(er).' The question to be asked is therefore the same as that raised by Johnson, who asked 'why, then, should the entire population be required to subsidise an activity that provides direct benefits only to the wealthiest segment?' (1984, p. 305). This immediately raises the issue of how such decisions are made; that is, whether they are based on majority voting (of individuals who are concerned only with their own marginal costs and benefits) or on social welfare considerations which may reflect an aversion to inequality.

The perspective generally taken in proposing the use of subsidies is that government subsidies towards higher education can be regarded as a form of investment in human capital. This investment yields, however, a negative (or at most very small positive) rate of return when viewed in narrow terms of the fiscal return to the government. The extra tax revenue arising from the increase in the tax base, which results from the associated increase in the number of individuals investing in higher education, is not usually thought to compensate for the investment expenditure. The various arguments mentioned briefly above are thus used to suggest that even with such a negative rate of return, investment is warranted because of the wider considerations which are relevant. However, some people have actually suggested that the rate of return may be quite substantial. For example, Holcombe and Holcombe (1984) have argued, in the context of the United States, that the government can invest $89 million to receive an annuity of $14.5 million for 40 years, giving a real rate of return of 15%. Hence investment 'makes sense even within the narrow framework of a wealth maximising government' (1984, p. 368). It seems most unlikely that this kind of argument would find wide support among economists, although some situations in which the rate of return may be positive are indicated in the following chapters.

The above arguments are not of course sufficient to argue either that governments *will* or *should* provide tax-financed subsidies. It is necessary to consider explicitly the decision-making mechanisms and the 'social evaluation' rules adopted, along with the costs of government intervention. For example, the subsidies must be financed from higher taxes (or borrowing, which involves higher future taxes) which may involve distortions that outweigh the benefits of the subsidies. There is a vast range of taxes and types of subsidy which may be considered and no general rule is available; each type of tax and subsidy scheme must be considered on its own merits. For a discussion of alternative forms of funding, see Barr (1993).

Faced with such a vast range of schemes which may be examined and the enormous complexity involved, this book focuses on a small number of aspects of higher education finance using a simplified model. The advantage of the model, in comparison with many earlier discussions, is that it attempts to allow both for the general equilibrium implications of the government's budget constraint and for the endogeneity of the government's decision. The book also focuses, as mentioned earlier, on the third type of rationale for tax-financed subsidies discussed above, that of external productivity effects. This is not to deny the potential importance of the other considerations; rather, it reflects the difficulty of handling all the issues simultaneously. Hence in what follows, capital market imperfections are ignored and individuals are assumed to be able to borrow as much as required at the fixed market rate of interest which is the same as that at which the government can borrow. The policy implications are of course quite different. For example, if imperfections in capital markets are regarded as the major issue, then student loans rather than direct grants (or tuition subsidies) are suggested. It would then be necessary to consider the range of problems associated with income-contingent loans, which may well involve some tax-financed subsidies.

As mentioned earlier, a wide range of tax and subsidy schemes is available. The simplest type of subsidy is an unconditional grant to all individuals wishing (and able) to invest in higher education, financed by an increase in the personal income tax. A much-neglected feature (at least in popular debates) of such grants is that they are not free from the point of view of recipients; they involve higher taxes over the working lives of recipients of the grants as well as those who do not invest. This gives rise to the important concept of a *deferred fee*. The deferred fee takes the form of a higher stream of tax payments than otherwise because taxes are higher than they would be without the grants, as a result of the government's budget constraint. It is thus possible, depending on the precise nature of the tax structure, for some very high income recipients to pay a total deferred fee which, in present value terms, exceeds their grant. Such individuals would vote for a reduced grant even though they benefit from higher education. Unconditional grants, even when combined with a progressive income tax schedule, will also increase lifetime inequality. Nevertheless, low-income individuals who do not invest, and who form a substantial majority of the population, may vote for a grant where the benefits to them, arising from the external effects of higher education, exceed the costs. The costs arise of course from the higher taxes, although the latter are mitigated to some extent by the higher tax base generated.

Another form of subsidy which may in practice exist alongside, or be carefully integrated with, a grant scheme involves the use of a government loan scheme. A zero real rate of interest applied to the loan provides a subsidy to all those who borrow, and simultaneously gives a slight advantage to those who repay more slowly. With an income-contingent schedule of repayments, those who repay slowly will be those with flatter and lower earnings profiles. This type of scheme must still have associated with it a deferred fee of the type mentioned above, but of course it will be smaller.

In Australia a combination of various systems is used. In addition to the AUSTUDY grant system, an income-contingent fee system was introduced in 1989, called the Higher Education Contribution Scheme (HECS). Payment of HECS charges range from 1 to 3 per cent of income per year, depending on the level of income, and there is a zero real rate of interest. An early study of this scheme was made by Chapman and Chia (1989) who, in a partial equilibrium analysis, examined the implications for the internal rate of return to higher education for individuals who are assumed to follow profiles of average earnings (for relevant occupational groups) over their working lives. In view of the low value of HECS charges, they found the impact to be very small. The charges have increased since their study.

This scheme was expanded in 1992 by the introduction of the AUS-TUDY Supplement, a form of income-contingent loan scheme (with the same repayment conditions as HECS) under which up to $2,000 per year of the AUSTUDY grant can be traded for $4,000 of loan. The implications of this new scheme were examined by Chapman and Harding (1993) who also calculated internal rates of return along average age–earnings profiles. Their study emphasized imperfect capital markets and the need for support systems to focus on those nearer the margin in order to avoid much of the regressivity of standard unconditional grants. However, they did not attempt to examine the distribution of rates of return.

Government and Individual Decisions

This book can be regarded as an exercise in mainstream public economics. The subject provides a good example of the basic point that in examining almost any issue in public economics it is necessary to consider the behaviour of all individuals and the government, and in particular to examine the circumstances in which actions are mutually consistent. The approach followed in this book assumes that individuals, in making their educational choice decision, attempt to maximize net lifetime income subject to constraints. The relevant constraints include their exogenously fixed 'ability' and the tax structure imposed by the government. The government is subject to a budget constraint; the tax system must generate the required revenue to finance higher education expenditure, given individuals' responses to the tax and subsidy system. Hence the framework must explicitly allow for these interdependencies.

The government is not satisfied merely to ensure that its budget constraint is met. This book examines two alternative types of government objective. The first approach assumes that the government carries out that tax and grant policy which is preferred by a majority of individuals. The second approach is one in which a conventional social welfare function, defined in terms of individuals' net lifetime incomes, is maximized. The use of an explicit form of social welfare function allows detailed comparisons between the two government objectives to be examined.

It is suggested that a public-choice approach to education provides some useful insights. An extensive argument for a public choice approach has been made by Majumdar (1983), and some empirical support found by Lovell (1978). Many aspects of public choice in education are examined in

Bowman (1986). Majority voting over taxes and fees for higher education has been modelled by Bös (1980), but his analysis is rather limited by the specification of education as a private consumption good which involves no forgone earnings. The present analysis treats higher education as an investment good requiring both direct costs and forgone earnings. However, it treats higher education as homogeneous, and abstracts from capital market imperfections and the risks associated with the investment.

In each case, of the public choice and social welfare approaches, the nature of the income tax system is taken as given, though of course the precise tax rates are endogenously determined. Hence the government is faced with a decision problem involving only one dimension. It is well known that public choices involving several variables are very complicated, though it might be argued that a more satisfactory approach would produce a model that is capable of examining the complete tax and transfer system simultaneously. While this point must be accepted at a very general level, it imposes an extremely severe requirement on the economic analysis and is therefore very seldom followed.

A further, more pragmatic, reason for separating the analysis along the lines followed in this book has also been suggested by Hare. He argued that a 'very practical' reason for such a separation

> is the simple observation that governments typically *do not* co-ordinate their spending and tax policies in the careful way that economic theory suggests they should. So it makes sense to think about, say, education policy in the presence of a given tax regime; and conversely we could analyse tax schedules given an education policy. Taken to its logical conclusion the combination of these partial optimisations would presumably yield some form of Nash equilibrium, which will normally differ from (and in welfare terms be inferior to) the overall social welfare optimum. However, in a particular institutional environment the Nash equilibrium may be the best attainable outcome.   (Hare, 1988, p. 76)

Hare's argument is therefore adopted for present purposes.

Some Interdependencies

Within a public choice-approach, the major question to be considered is as follows: Under what circumstances would a majority of individuals be prepared to vote for a proportion of the cost of higher education per person to be met from tax revenue, given that the majority will not find it worthwhile to invest in education? The analysis is restricted to a single cohort of individuals. This is not meant to deny that inter-generational issues are relevant, but they do introduce additional highly complex problems. The discussion is therefore offered as the first stage in a more complete analysis.

Each individual in the cohort may be supposed to have an exogenously determined endowment of ability both to obtain income if uneducated and to benefit from further education. The assumption that these two types of ability are perfectly corrrelated provides another important simplification which avoids the need to examine individuals' choices in terms of their comparative advantages. It is not necessary for present purposes to specify precisely what constitutes income-earning ability, though it may be regarded as some kind of combination of many separate factors, including family background. Those with a higher endowment are assumed to obtain a relatively higher income even if they are not educated, and to obtain a relatively higher increase in earnings if they become educated.

The educational choice decision is based on an assessment by each individual of the net present value of lifetime earnings. Important factors in this calculation are the direct private cost of education and the nature of the tax system, in addition to the perceived earnings that result from higher education. The cost of education includes both forgone earnings while individuals delay entry into the labour market and any fee which must be paid. If the level of fees is substantial, then as mentioned earlier an interesting question arises of the influence of imperfect capital markets, but for present purposes it is assumed that individuals can freely borrow at a fixed rate of interest that is the same as the lending rate and the government's borrowing rate.

Education will be less desirable to the extent that the tax system is more progressive and average tax rates are higher. Both these factors will reduce the effective rate of return to higher education. In view of the assumption that the income-earning ability and the ability of individuals to benefit from higher education are correlated, there will be, for any tax system and education cost structure, some endowment level below which it is not worthwhile investing in higher education. This level may be called the *educational choice margin*. An individual at the margin will expect the same net lifetime earnings whether educated or not. Assume for the time being that higher education is not subject to rationing, so that in effect the supply is demand-determined. The introduction of rationing does not affect the major argument, and for this reason the analysis of its effects is delayed until later.

It is worth stressing here that this book does not examine a model in which individuals' labour supplies are affected by the income tax system, other than the effect of income taxes on the incentive to invest in higher education. Individuals do not respond continuously to variations in the tax rate, as only changes which affect the investment decision influence labour supply when entry into the labour market is delayed. The complications involved in introducing learning into a multi-period optimal tax model are

illustrated by Brunner (1986). Atkinson and Stiglitz (1980) examine a much
simpler model in which the tax rate affects the time spent by individuals in
general education. Hence there is a larger effect of tax changes on labour
supply in their model because all individuals respond continuously to tax
rate changes rather than make a discrete choice.

The Introduction of a Grant

In considering the various interdependencies it is useful to begin from a
situation in which all higher education costs are met from fees imposed on
those who invest in it, so that taxation is only required to finance non-
education government expenditure. Suppose that a policy is introduced
whereby each educated individual has to pay only a specified proportion of
the full fee, while the remainder of the cost is met through the income tax
system. It may be supposed that each individual receives an unconditional
government grant to pay a proportion of the required fee. This grant may
be allowed to exceed the value of the fee; for example it may include a
maintenance component.

The first effect of the introduction of the grant is that the educational
choice margin will fall. Those who were just below the old margin find it
worthwhile to invest in higher education because a component of the cost of
investing has fallen. This reduction in the choice margin has several
implications. First, the partial financing of education through the tax
system means that tax rates must be adjusted if deficit neutrality is to be
maintained; that is, income tax revenue must be increased to match the
extra expenditure above that required for non-education purposes. To the
extent that the tax system is progressive, the burden of the additional tax
will fall relatively more on those with higher earnings, who are largely those
who receive the private returns from education. Even with a proportional
tax system, the educated will pay more in taxation than they would pay
when there is no grant.

It is therefore important to recognize that the grant is not 'free', although
repayment of all or part of it is deferred until educated individuals enter the
labour force. Most individuals above the educational choice margin will
probably pay an extra amount of tax over their working life with a present
value that is below the value of the grant. But for those with very high
endowments it is possible that the present value of the extra tax payments
exceeds the value of the grant, especially with a progressive tax structure.
The increase in taxation, required to finance the grant, will modify to some
extent the 'initial' or 'first round' effect of the grant in reducing the
educational choice margin. A further possibility resulting from the reduction in the educational choice margin is that, because of the increase in the

supply of more highly skilled workers and the reduction in the supply of less-skilled workers, the relative wages of those who invest in higher education will fall. In this case those who receive the grant, but would otherwise invest in higher education anyway, are forced to bear a further cost.

Majority Support for a Grant

The majority of individuals are expected to be below the educational choice margin. Hence it is necessary to consider why a majority would be prepared to support the use of a grant system rather than full fee-paying, especially as the above argument shows that they will be faced with higher taxes. This is where further types of interdependence become relevant. As already discussed, a consequence of the reduction in the educational choice margin is that more people invest in higher education. Given that investment in education leads to higher earnings over the working life, the introduction of a grant has the effect of increasing the tax base. It is also possible that an increase in the number of highly educated individuals will have the effect of reducing some private rates of return to higher education. Nevertheless the tax base will increase, and this mitigates against any rise in taxes caused by the need to finance the grants through the tax system.

The above argument still does not explain why the non-educated majority would vote in favour of a grant system. If the grant could be concentrated only on those who would otherwise be just below the educational choice margin, it is possible that the 'tax base' effect could outweigh the cost of the grant, but in the case of unconditional benefits this is extremely unlikely, as argued earlier. However, the existence of external effects implies that the marginal benefit may exceed the marginal cost of an increase in the grant for those who do not invest in higher education. Suppose, as mentioned above, that the increase in the number of people with higher education results in a general increase in productivity such that *all* individuals benefit from an increase in earnings. In addition to the increase in aggregate earnings arising from the private returns to investment, there is thus an additional general growth resulting from the externality. There may also be non-pecuniary external effects but, as explained earlier, these are ignored here. Majority support for the use of tax-financed grants for higher education depends on the extent of this social as well as private return.

The literature on external effects is not very clear about the precise nature of such benefits. Suppose, however, that the general rate of increase in earnings is higher, the higher is the proportion of the population educated, although decreasing returns may be expected. The reduction in the educational choice margin that results directly from an increase in the grant will also lead to a higher growth of earnings that is shared by all individuals, irrespective of their educational status. If this effect is combined with that of the higher tax base resulting from private returns, there is a possibility that an increase in the grant can ultimately raise the net lifetime income of the uneducated, even if they also pay more tax. However, the argument suggests that the existence of a positive externality arising from higher education is not sufficient to generate majority support for the use of tax-financed grants; the general growth rate of earnings experienced by everyone as a result of productivity gains must outweigh the effects of the higher taxation.

The assumption that the general increase in productivity is related to the proportion of individuals investing in higher education has implications for the use of merit-based grants or scholarships. From the point of view of those below the educational choice margin, concern is with the *marginal* benefits and costs of an increase in the tax-financed grant. The use of a grant which is available only to those with very high ability, and who would anyway invest in higher education, would have very little to recommend it. The grant should, where possible, be concentrated on those close to the margin unless, of course, a very different view about the source of external effects is taken. A similar point has been made by Baum and Schwartz (1988).

The above discussion has shown that when allowance is made for a number of important interdependencies, there is nothing very surprising about the suggestion that the majority of individuals may support some form of grant for higher education, even though they will not themselves benefit directly from education. However, this kind of general discussion cannot establish the precise level of the grant, in relation to the cost per educated individual, that would be supported by the majority. Further analysis requires the use of a more detailed model. The examination of such a model provides the main focus of this book. A non-technical introduction to the model and discussion of some of its properties is given in the following section.

1.2   A SIMPLE FRAMEWORK OF ANALYSIS

The Investment Decision

In order to simplify the analysis, higher education is regarded purely as an investment good so that there are no perceived consumption benefits. Furthermore, the analysis will abstract from differences between academic subjects so that higher education is regarded simply as a homogeneous good. These assumptions are obviously unrealistic but are unlikely to influence the major results of the analysis. However, investment requires not only direct costs in the form of fees but also a period of full-time study. This obviously implies that forgone earnings during the period of study form a further important component of the cost. This contrasts with the model of Johnson (1984) who assumes that higher education is undertaken instantaneously. The additional simplification is made that all individuals who invest in higher education will automatically graduate; thus a degree is regarded simply as providing an attendance certificate. However, this does not mean that all individuals benefit equally from the investment, just as all individuals do not have the same forgone earnings during the period of full time study. There is a distribution of ability, in terms of the ability both to obtain income in the labour market and the ability to benefit from higher education. These types of ability are, as discussed earlier, thus assumed to be perfectly correlated. The attendance certificate given on graduation may be thought to provide an assessment of the individual's performance, on a continuous scale, and this will be related to the ability level. The practical question of whether or not higher education imparts useful cognitive skills or is simply a rather expensive form of screening device is thus simply by-passed by the assumption that it is indeed an investment in the acquisition of productive skills.

The investment decision can usefully be considered using a diagram in which net lifetime income, V, is measured on the vertical axis and ability, y, is measured on the horizontal axis, as in Figure 1.1. Consider a single cohort of individuals within which the distribution of ability is given exogenously. For those who do not invest in higher education, the relationship between net lifetime income and ability may be reflected by the profile marked V^N. This starts at the origin, and since ability is regarded as reflecting income-earning ability (following some appropriate transformation), the line V^N will be a straight line if there is a proportional tax system, or somewhat concave, depending on the progressivity of the income tax schedule.

The profile for those who invest in higher education is shown as V^E. This will start below the origin, because the direct costs (despite the low forgone earnings) outweigh the gains for such low-ability individuals. Beyond some point, the gains outweigh the costs and V^E becomes positive. If the benefit from higher education (in terms of the extent to which earnings during the working life are higher than they would otherwise be) is positively related to ability, y, then the profile V^E will be convex. This convexity is not likely to be outweighed by any tax progressivity. There is therefore a single point, E, at which the two lines cross, corresponding to an ability level of y^*. This level is the *educational choice margin*. All those with ability in excess of this

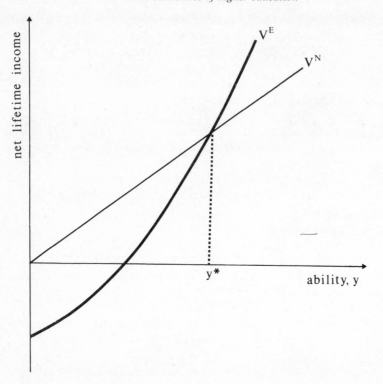

Figure 1.1   The educational choice margin

level will find it worthwhile to invest in higher education. Furthermore, the schedules will only cross once (at least for feasible, that is non-negative, values) so that y^* is unique.

The above explanation has been somewhat over-simplified, since it has ignored the possibility of external effects arising from the fact that a proportion of the cohort invests in higher education. Two influences have already been discussed briefly. First, there is a *tax base effect*, since the earnings of those who invest are higher than otherwise so that any given net government revenue can be raised with lower tax rates. Secondly, there is a *productivity effect* arising from the complementarity between skill levels. Both these effects themselves depend on the educational choice margin, y^*. This means that the profiles shown in Figure 1.1 must be regarded as being mutually consistent with that value of y^* given by their intersection; the two-dimensional nature of the diagram is not sufficient to capture the full extent of the interdependencies involved. However, it will be shown later that for proportional taxes the choice margin is independent of the productivity effect.

The educational choice margin depends therefore on a variety of factors, but it is useful to consider the partial relationship between y^* and the marginal tax rate, t. The relationship is referred to as the *educational choice schedule*. For the time being it is probably best to think of a proportional tax system in which all income is taxed at the same fixed rate. The relationship between the educational choice margin and the tax rate may be expected to take the kind of shape illustrated in Figure 1.2. As the tax rate approaches unity, it is not worthwhile for anyone to invest in higher education, whatever their ability level, so that this educational choice schedule will asymptotically approach the horizontal line at $t = 1$. The precise shape and position of the choice schedule depends on the other factors, such as the nature of the private returns to investment, the extent of the external effect, the size of the grant, and the amount of government revenue which needs to be raised for other purposes.

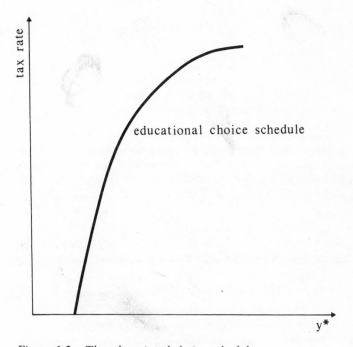

Figure 1.2   The educational choice schedule

The Government Budget Constraint

It is also very important to consider the constraint imposed on government choices, since any higher education grant must be financed from tax

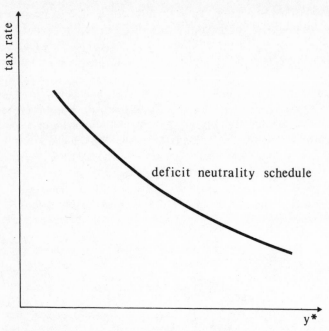

Figure 1.3   The deficit neutrality schedule

revenue. It is useful, as with educational choice, to consider the partial relationship between the required tax rate and the educational choice margin. As the choice margin falls, with other parameters held constant, the associated increase in the proportion of the cohort that invests in higher education (and thus receives the grant) means that government expenditure must increase. This expenditure is financed by raising the tax rate t, so that the relationship is expected to be downward-sloping from left to right, as shown in Figure 1.3. This relationship is most appropriately referred to as a *deficit neutrality schedule*. This is because the total revenue raised from the income tax varies along the length of the schedule, but with a transfer system (the higher education grant) the net revenue is held constant. This net revenue may or may not be associated with an overall budget deficit.

As mentioned earlier, the extent of the tax change is mitigated to some extent by the increase in the tax base. This in turn depends both on the private returns to investment and the external productivity effect which benefits even those who do not invest. The schedule is therefore expected to be relatively flat, particularly for relatively high values of y^*. This slope is to some extent also related to the form of the distribution of ability, y. If this distribution is positively skewed, then reductions in y^* which take place in the right-hand tail of the distribution of y will have a smaller effect on the number of individuals who are induced to invest, thereby causing a smaller increase in the required expenditure.

Equilibrium Combinations

The situation whereby, for a given set of parameters, the higher education choices of individuals, made subject to a given tax structure, are consistent with the government's satisfaction of its budget constraint, is given by the intersection between the educational choice schedule and the deficit neutrality schedule. Given the equilibrium combinations of the tax rate, t, and the educational choice margin, y^*, the net lifetime incomes of all individuals are determined.

There is one implication of this type of equilibrium which is worth stressing. At the educational choice margin, the rate of return from investing in higher education is equal to the rate of interest at which all individuals (and the government) lend and borrow. Above the margin, however, there is a *distribution* of rates of return. In examining the comparative statics of alternative policies, it is important to find what happens to those near the margin, since the investment decisions of those who are well above or below the eduational choice margin are unlikely to be affected by changes. The implications for those near to the margin may not be reflected in changes in, for example, the arithmetic mean rate of return or some other measure of location of the complete distribution of rates of return. Despite the existence of the distribution of rates, empirical studies usually attempt to estimate a single value of some rate of return to higher education, based on average earnings profiles. The value of such single measures is not very clear, but there is an additional empirical problem.

Within the present framework the calculation of some kind of rate of return based on the average earnings profiles of the two groups, those observed to be above and those below the educational choice margin, would be highly misleading as an indication of private rates of return to investment. The differences between the two averages in each period reflect the distribution of ability as well as the effect of higher education. Empirical estimates will thus be highly spurious (and biased upwards) if they ignore the interaction between ability and education. The problem is of course that it is not possible to observe directly what individuals would have earned if they had not invested in higher education. The failure to allow for this problem in many studies was also pointed out by Blaug (1989).

Any equilibrium represented by a point of intersection between a deficit neutrality schedule and an educational choice schedule will be a feasible position with mutual consistency between all individuals' plans and with the government's budget constraint satisfied. However, it is reasonable to suppose that the government has some objective of its own, rather than simply aiming for consistency. This book examines the government's choice of higher education grant under two assumptions about its objective. First, the government is assumed to select the policy which is preferred by a simple majority of individuals: the problem is one of considering the public choice of grant under majority voting. Secondly, the government is assumed to maximize a conventional social welfare function defined in terms of individuals' net lifetime incomes. In each case the choice of just a single variable, the level of the higher education grant, is considered, with the appropriate tax rate adjusted accordingly.

1.3   A MAJORITY VOTING EQUILIBRIUM

Majority Voting with Proportional Taxation

Consider the variation in the net lifetime income of individuals as the level of the tax-financed grant is gradually increased. Such a relationship defines the *preference profile* of each individual. Those who have very high ability levels would invest in higher education even if there were no grant. As the grant increases, they will benefit as recipients of this transfer, but their lifetime taxation will also increase. Initially the extra grant (combined with external effects) may be expected to outweigh the extra tax costs for such individuals, so that their preference profiles will be upward-sloping. Beyond some level of the grant, however, the extra tax cost will outweigh the marginal benefit, leading the preference profiles to turn downwards.

Those with lower ability levels may not find it worthwhile to invest when the grant is very low. However, their net lifetime incomes may at first rise as the grant is increased, as a result of the external productivity effects from which they benefit, but will again fall as the tax cost outweighs the benefits of further increases. Nevertheless, as the grant is increased further, such individuals may at some point find it worthwhile to invest in higher education, when they will be direct recipients of the grant. The implication of this kind of variation is that such individuals will be expected to have double-peaked preferences for the grant. However, those with very low ability levels will never find it worthwhile to invest so that they, like the high-ability people, are expected to have single-peaked preferences. An example of a preference profile is shown in Figure 1.4.

A well-known result of public choice theory is that if all individuals have single-peaked preferences, a stable majority voting equilibrium exists in which the median voter dominates – the median voter being identified as the person whose peak of the preference profiles is in the middle. Given the

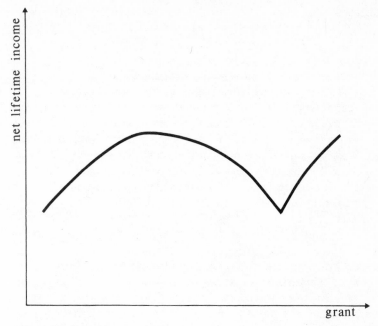

Figure 1.4   Preference profiles

single-peakedness of the profiles, the alignment of individuals remains unchanged as the choice variable varies, so that coalitions between those on either side of the median will not form and the median voter's preferences dominate. If, however, preference profiles are not all single-peaked, as in the present context, there is not necessarily a majority voting equilibrium; 'cyclical' voting can result in which social choices appear to be intransitive even though all individuals have consistent preferences. The existence of double-peaked preferences for a higher education grant therefore raises potentially serious problems for the analysis of majority choices. Fortunately, it can be shown that a stable equilibrium exists in the special case of proportional taxation.

If the income tax is proportional, it can be demonstrated that all those who are below the educational choice margin agree about the level of the grant which maximizes their net lifetime incomes. Their preference profiles have their first peak at the same grant level, even if some profiles may turn upwards at very high grant levels. This is essentially because, with a proportional tax, net lifetime income for those below y^*, as shown by V^N in Figure 1.1, is simply proportional to their ability level. Hence in maximizing V^N with respect to the grant level, even after allowing for the various interdependencies involved, the level of ability is irrelevant. Given that in any realistic case, significantly less than 50 per cent of individuals invest in higher education, there will not be a problem about finding a majority voting equilibrium. The median voter may be identified simply as the individual with median ability level.

Given the type of non-linear relationship between net lifetime income and ability, shown by V^E in Figure 1.1, maximization with respect to the level of the grant will clearly produce a first-order condition in which the ability level does not cancel. Hence those above the margin, y^*, are not unanimous in their choice of grant size but, as explained above, they are a minority. This diversity of views among those who invest in higher education contrasts with the model of Johnson (1984), in which 'all members of the bright segment of the population will have the same opinion about what the tuition subsidy rate should be' (p. 306).

The important question also arises of whether there can be more than one majority voting equilibrium value of the grant, given the highly non-linear nature of the model. Could there be a low grant and low tax equilibrium, along with a high grant and high tax equilibrium? The existence of two equilibria would present awkward analytical problems, especially in considering the comparative static characteristics of the model. For example, a small change in an exogenous variable may lead to a large discrete jump in the majority choice of the grant. However, such multiple equilibria are ruled out by the requirement that less than 50 per cent of the population invests in higher education. Any attempt to extend the approach, to deal with a context in which those who do not invest can possibly form a minority, must pay serious attention to the possibility of more than one equilibrium position.

Some Comparative Statics

In the proportional tax case discussed above, the majority voting equilibrium value of the grant is given by that grant for which the marginal cost of a grant increase just balances the marginal benefit, for any individual not investing in higher education, remembering that all those below the educational choice margin are unanimous in their choice of preferred grant. The marginal cost reflects the extra tax which must be paid, resulting from the extra grant to those already investing, and the additional tax cost resulting from the drop in the educational choice margin. The latter depends on the relative position of the choice margin in the ability distribution, the shape of that distribution, and the extent to which the tax base is altered. The marginal benefit depends on the external effect which leads to an increase in productivity and thus an increase in the incomes of everyone. This in turn depends on the relationship between the external effect and the proportion investing in higher education (which is expected to be concave), and therefore also on the form of the ability distribution at the choice margin. The marginal benefit of increasing the grant will fall as the grant increases (so long as the individual remains below the educational choice margin), while the marginal cost will rise, so that a unique equilibrium is expected. The effects of any exogenous changes may be examined by considering how the change is likely to affect these marginal costs and benefits to those below the educational choice margin.

Suppose the net revenue required by the government increases, resulting from an increase in expenditure on non-education-related goods and services. Assume for simplicity that this increase has no indirect effects on the earnings of individuals or the returns from higher education. The effect of the increase in expenditure is thus to leave the educational choice schedule unchanged, but to shift the deficit neutrality schedule vertically upwards, as shown in Figure 1.5. This leads unambiguously to a rise in the choice margin, y^*, and a rise in the tax rate, t. The rise in the educational choice margin is associated with a fall in the proportion investing and therefore also with a fall in the external benefit, and consequently a fall in

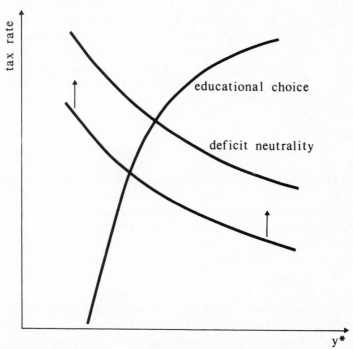

Figure 1.5   An increase in non-education expenditure

the tax base. Given the assumed concavity in the relationship between the external benefit and the proportion investing in higher education, the marginal benefit of an increase in the grant is increased, with little effect on the marginal cost. Although the absolute value of the tax rate is higher, in order to finance the extra non-educational expenditure, it is the *marginal* cost of increasing the grant which is relevant here. The net effect is therefore that the exogenous increase in government spending leads to an endogenous increase in the majority choice of the grant, and therefore a further increase in the tax rate. The obvious implication is that if the government is cutting non-education expenditure, for whatever reason, the majority choice also favours cuts in higher education spending through a cut in the grant.

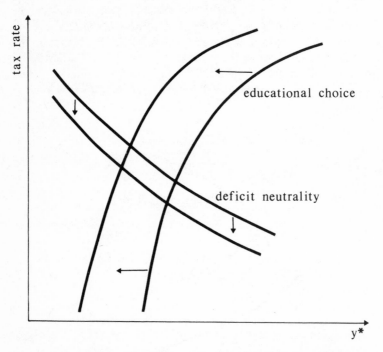

Figure 1.6   An increase in the private benefits of higher education

Consider next an increase in the private benefits from higher education, reflecting higher rates of return at all ability levels. The effect on the two schedules is illustrated in Figure 1.6. The educational choice schedule shifts leftwards reflecting the greater attraction of higher education, while the deficit neutrality schedule shifts downwards reflecting the higher tax base associated with any given value of y^*. The net effect on the tax rate is therefore unclear at this stage, although the choice margin is expected to fall. The associated increase in the proportion investing leads to a decrease in the marginal benefit to those below y^* of an increase in the grant. The net result is not unambiguous. Further analysis therefore requires the use of a model with much more specification. It will be shown in later chapters that the most likely effect is that the fall in the marginal benefit will dominate any change in the marginal cost, implying that higher private returns lead to a fall in the majority choice of grant. In order to establish this result clearly, it is necessary to add further structure to the simple model.

Suppose next that there is an increase in the external benefit resulting from the complementarity between the groups in production. This does not affect the educational choice schedule, where the income tax is proportional, but the deficit neutrality schedule shifts downwards because of the effect on the tax base. This is shown in Figure 1.7, where it can be seen that the educational choice margin and the tax rate fall, although the former reduction is relatively small given the steepness of the choice schedule over the range shown. If the proportional tax rate, t, is initially high then of course there will be a larger effect on the margin, y^*. The marginal benefit of raising the grant is reduced while the marginal cost falls.

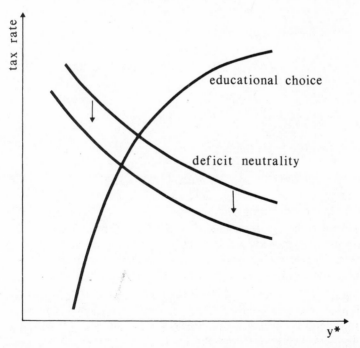

Figure 1.7   An increase in the external effects of higher education

The final result is again not entirely clear without further structure being imposed on the model. However, it will be seen that the likely result is an endogenous increase in the grant preferred by the majority. This means that the reduction in the marginal costs outweighs the reduction in the marginal benefit of raising the grant.

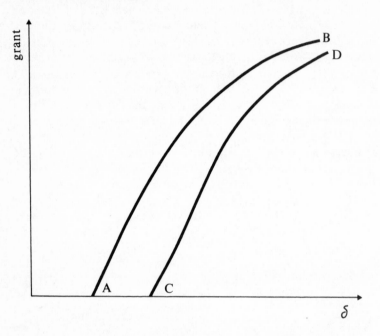

Figure 1.8   Variations in the grant and external effects

It is worth stressing again the point mentioned at the beginning of this chapter, that the mere existence of an external benefit does not by itself guarantee majority support for a positive grant. The benefit must be sufficiently large so that it outweighs the cost of the grant which is imposed on those not directly benefiting. In later chapters of this book the external benefit will be specified as a concave function of the proportion of the cohort investing in higher education, with the function depending on just one parameter. This is very convenient, since an increase in the externality can then be modelled simply as an increase in the relevant parameter. The general form of the relationship between the majority choice of grant and the external effect is illustrated in Figure 1.8 in which the grant is measured on the vertical axis and the parameter governing the extent of the external effect (for a given educational choice margin) is measured on the horizontal axis. The upper schedule *AB* is for a higher level of non-education expenditure than for the schedule marked *CD*, given the above comparative static result. Neither of these schedules begins at the origin.

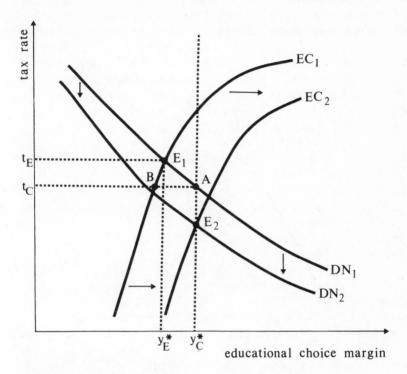

Figure 1.9   Quantity rationing

A Supply Constraint

It has been assumed above that the supply of higher education is demand-determined, but the argument can easily be adapted to allow for an upper limit to the proportion of the cohort able to invest in higher education. This restriction is translated into a lower limit to the educational choice margin. Consider Figure 1.9 and suppose that the educational choice schedule EC_1 and the deficit neutrality schedule DN_1 result from the unconstrained value of the grant that is preferred by the majority of the cohort. This produces an equilibrium choice margin and tax rate of y_E^* and t_E respectively at the intersection, E_1, of the two schedules. Now suppose that an effective supply constraint is imposed so that the minimum value of y^* allowed is y_c^*. The actual tax required to finance this choice margin, at the initial uncon-strained value of the grant, is thus t_c and the excess demand for higher education is represented by the distance AB. This distance does not of course measure the excess demand directly, since the number of individuals associated with any given educational choice margin depends on the shape of the distribution of ability.

The non-educated majority can at most receive external benefits from having the choice margin of y_c^*, so there is simply no point in subsidizing the educated to such an extent that there is an excess demand. A lower value of the grant shifts the educational choice schedule to the right while the deficit neutrality schedule shifts downwards. The preferred (constrained) value of the grant is therefore that value giving the schedules EC_2 and DN_2. In this case the intersection at E_2 gives rise to a demand for higher education that is consistent with the constrained supply. Even if the external effects of higher education are significant, a supply constraint has the effect of imposing an upper limit on the value of the grant preferred by the majority. The analysis in the remainder of this book will continue to assume that there is not a binding supply constraint, but it is worth bearing the implications of such a constraint in mind.

A Progressive Income Tax

The existence of a progressive income tax means that those with relatively low incomes, below the educational choice margin, can 'shift' relatively more of the cost of raising the grant to those with high incomes. If there is a tax-free threshold, which is typical of a progressive tax, then those below the threshold effectively have a zero marginal cost of increasing the grant if the resulting external benefit does not raise their income above the threshold. Consequently, the people with very low incomes may align themselves with those just above the educational choice margin in being in favour of a grant increase. Similarly, those slightly below the margin may agree with the very high-income individuals in preferring to see a grant reduction. Hence the problem of establishing a majority voting equilibrium is much more complicated than in the proportional tax case. The majority of individuals, those below the choice margin, are no longer unanimous. It does not seem possible to establish the general existence of a voting equilibrium with double-peaked preferences in this case, unlike the proportional tax case. However, when more structure is added to the model it is possible to examine the detailed preference profiles of various percentiles of the distribution of ability, and establish an equilibrium majority voting outcome.

It has already been mentioned that the major focus of this book concerns the choice of higher education grant, for a given tax system, though the tax rate itself is endogenous. However, the existence of a tax-free threshold, combined with the fact that investment in higher education involves significant forgone earnings, implies that there may be situations in which some individuals, who otherwise have relatively high lifetime earnings, may not pay any income tax during earlier years. This in turn raises the possibility that a relatively high-income individual may prefer to see an increase in the tax-free threshold while a relatively lower-income individual, not investing in higher education, would benefit from a reduction in the threshold. Such an apparently paradoxical result would raise problems for majority voting over the income tax structure, *given* the value of the higher education grant.

The present context is really just one example of a situation in which some individuals are able to shift income between periods. An important result concerning the public choice of a progressive tax system in a single period context was established by Roberts (1977). He showed that a majority voting equilibrium exists, despite the double-peakedness of preferences, if the ranking or ordering of individuals is not affected by the tax system. It is therefore useful to use the higher education framework of this book in order to investigate the issue of public choice over progressive taxation. It will be seen that the very convenient result established by Roberts does not extend to the multi-period case where there is a tax-free threshold and individuals have the ability to shift income between periods.

1.4   SOCIAL WELFARE

A Grant and Inequality

The previous section has concentrated on the situation where the government is assumed to impose the grant that is preferred by a simple majority of the cohort. Each individual has also been assumed to be concerned only with net lifetime income, with no regard to the situation faced by others. Hence no single individual has any concern for the degree of inequality in the cohort. Given the assumed link between income-earning ability and the ability to benefit from higher education, the higher education grant is unambiguously regressive in that it increases the inequality of net lifetime income, however measured. Given that net government revenue (for non-education purposes) is held constant when the grant is increased, there is no need to distinguish between the effects relating to the *disproportionality* of tax and benefit payments and their effect on income *inequality*. Furthermore, the ranking of individuals (by net lifetime income) is independent of the grant level. Hence it is sufficient to concentrate on the effects of various alternatives on the inequality of net income. Since an increase in the grant is associated with an increase in inequality, the question arises of how the majority choice of grant compares with that resulting from the maximization of a social welfare function which reflects a degree of aversion to inequality.

The Trade-off Between Equity and 'Efficiency'

An increase in the level of the grant is, as mentioned above, associated with an increase in inequality. However, as a result of the tax-base effect and the externality, generating higher real incomes for everyone, an increase in the grant will, over a certain range of values, be associated with an increase in the arithmetic mean net lifetime income of the cohort. A stage will nevertheless ultimately be reached when there are so many people receiving the grant that the concavity of the relationship between the externality and the proportion investing in higher education, combined with the smaller increase in the tax base as more of the lower-ability people invest, means that arithmetic mean lifetime income begins to decline. This combination of a falling mean income with an increase in inequality is unequivocally bad, given the very general assumption about the social welfare function. Hence the range of grants producing this result can be ruled out. The general type of relationship between lifetime income and inequality is shown in Figure 1.10 as the line *ABC*.

It is most convenient to restrict attention to those types of social welfare function which can be expressed in 'abbreviated' form. This means that social welfare can be written as a function of arithmetic mean net lifetime income and a measure of inequality; for a detailed treatment of such functions, see Lambert (1993). In this case there is no difficulty in considering a trade-off between equity and average income, often referred to in rather loose terms as a trade-off between equity and efficiency. In terms of Figure 1.10 the social welfare function is described by a set of social indifference curves which are upward-sloping from left to right. If the social welfare function has no aversion to inequality, then the point *B* will be chosen because this maximizes average net income and social indifference curves are horizontal, otherwise the optimal position is one of tangency between an upward-sloping social indifference curve and the constraint *ABC*. Such a tangency position is illustrated as point *T* in Figure 1.10, along the indifference curve *W*. At this level of generality it is not clear how the choice of grant resulting from maximization of the social welfare function compares with the majority choice; all that can be said is that it will depend to some extent on the degree of inequality aversion of the welfare function. Hence further comparisons require the use of a more fully specified model.

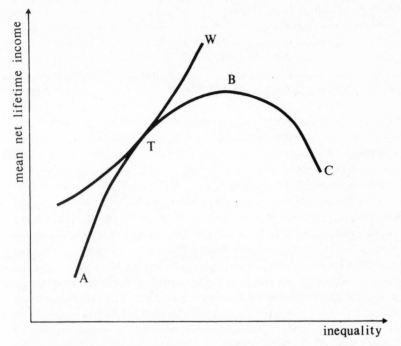

Figure 1.10   The trade-off between equity and efficiency

1.5   OUTLINE OF THE BOOK

The previous sections have attempted to give a non-technical introduction to the issues examined in this book and the type of model used. Later chapters concentrate on more detailed analyses. Before starting the formal modelling, however, Chapter 2 briefly discusses some of the previous literature, particularly that concerned with the external effects of higher education and the effects of subsidies on inequality. In view of the vast range of earlier studies in the general area, no attempt has been made to provide a detailed survey. Rather, the purpose is to place the present approach in some context, particularly as the kind of modelling carried out in later chapters abstracts from many aspects which those interested in the economics of higher education have emphasized. The aim, as discussed earlier, is to take a public finance perspective and explore a model which is capable of handling a number of potentially important interdependencies which are often ignored.

Chapter 3 explores some of the interdependencies within a rather more general model; that is, one which does not use explicit functional forms for some of the important relationships. The emphasis is on majority voting over the level of a higher education grant, and the treatment of comparative static properties of the model. It is seen that, even within a simple model, the interdependencies are extensive and considerably complicate the formal analysis of comparative statics. Furthermore, the qualitative analysis of changes is quite limited in that the direction of change of few of the relevant endogenous variables, particularly the level of grant, can be predicted *a priori*. It therefore seems that much more structure needs to be added to the model in order to provide unambiguous comparative statics using numerical analyses.

Chapter 4 therefore adds much more structure to the model. In particular, the educational choice schedule and deficit neutrality schedule, discussed in general terms above, are derived in detail. The chapter restricts attention to a proportional income tax and majority voting equilibria for the size of grant. It is found that, even using simple specifications, the model is highly non-linear, so that iterative numerical methods have to be used to solve the model.

Chapter 5 extends the analysis to include a progressive income tax. It also considers the maximization of a social welfare function and contrasts the results with the use of majority voting. The income tax function used has a single marginal tax rate applied to incomes measured in excess of a tax-free threshold. Chapter 5 also considers the different question of individuals' preferences over the tax schedule, for a given higher education grant, as mentioned above.

Chapter 6 continues the theme of the end of Chapter 5, that is the choice of progressive tax schedule, in terms of the choice of the tax-free threshold. The apparently paradoxical result that some relatively high-income individuals may prefer to see an increase in the tax-free threshold, while some relatively lower-income individuals would prefer to see the threshold fall, is examined using a much simpler model. It is found that Roberts's (1977) result on the choice of progressive taxation in a single period cannot be extended to the multi-period case with a tax-free threshold if, as in the present context, individuals are able to alter the time stream of their earnings by investing in higher education.

Chapter 7 returns to the question of majority voting of the higher education grant in the context of a proportional income tax. However, the model is extended to allow for the existence of social transfers which are means-tested. Furthermore, the chapter explores the use of means-testing of the higher education grant, which allows higher education expenditure to be concentrated on those near to the educational choice margin. Chapter 7 also examines the implications of alternative schemes for lifetime inequality. It shows that allowing for the endogeneity of the higher education grant has important implications for judging the effects of exogenous changes in other areas.

Finally, Chapter 8 examines the use of a tax surcharge as a further means of financing grants. This takes the form of an addition to the marginal tax rate applied to those who invest in higher education. It therefore differs from an income-contingent loan scheme since there is no requirement that the grant be fully repaid. It is found that the introduction of a tax surcharge is associated with an increase in the grant which is approved by a majority of the cohort; this is not surprising, since it lowers the marginal cost, facing those who do not invest, of raising the grant. More interesting is the result that, while the rate of return to the very high-income earners falls, those close to the educational choice margin experience an increase in the rate of return. This clearly demonstrates the need to examine the distribution of rates of return, rather than concentrating on a single value as in the vast majority of empirical studies.

2. Some previous studies

The purpose of this chapter is to take a very brief and selective look at earlier related studies. Some references to this literature have already been made in Chapter 1 and need not be repeated here. Section 2.1 discusses some related models of higher education finance, while section 2.2 is concerned with external effects and their measurement. Some aspects of the extensive debate on the redistributive effects of higher education subsidies are discussed in section 2.3, where studies are distinguished according to their basic approach to the measurement of redistribution.

2.1 HIGHER EDUCATION MODELS

There is of course a huge literature on the economies of education generally, but the number of studies which take a public finance perspective and which also concentrate on higher education is relatively small. Reference has already been made to the brief discussion by Atkinson and Stiglitz (1980) which helps to illustrate some of the issues in optimal taxation in the context of tax-financed transfer payments. A useful analytical survey of the public economics of education finance is provided by Hare (1988). The advantage of Hare's approach is that he begins with a very general model and carefully discusses the components of that model and the way in which different authors have added more 'structure' in order to derive results.

The present study, as outlined in the previous chapter, focuses on the endogeneity of the government's choice of the level of a grant to those undertaking higher education, using social welfare and public-choice approaches. A full-length study of the value of taking a public-choice perspective has been provided by Majumdar (1983). Theoretical analysis of the willingness of a majority to support the funding of higher education through the tax system have been considered by previous writers, using rather different approaches to that considered here. For example, Bös (1980) produces a median voter model of the demand for education. However, he does not consider education as an investment but models it as a private consumption good. Furthermore, individuals can consume different levels of education simply by buying more education at the given fee. The state's costs are met from a progressive system of taxation and the remaining individual costs are levied on the educated in the form of fees. Under a progressive tax system, and with a positively skewed distribution of incomes, public provision not surprisingly involves redistribution towards the median voter. A further result is that the median voter's choice of subsidy increases when the level of non-education government expenditure increases. Despite the differences between the models, the same result is found in the present study.

Reference has been made to the different approach taken in the important paper by Johnson (1984), who develops a model where education increases skills and earning capacity but, as in Bös's model, there is no opportunity cost in terms of forgone earnings. Johnson argues that those with low ability, and who do not find it directly profitable to invest in education, can benefit from a subsidy towards the cost of educating the more able if there is complementarity between skills in the production process.

Johnson divides the population into three groups according to their ability; the groups are low, medium and highly skilled. The medium-skilled can become highly skilled workers by investing in education but the low-skilled cannot improve on their skill level. If there are productivity gains to the low-skilled which arise from an increase in the number of high-skilled workers, the low-skilled will benefit indirectly from subsidies towards the cost of educating medium-skilled workers. The cost to the low-skilled workers, in the form of higher taxes, of inducing the medium-skilled to invest in their own education is compared with the productivity (and hence wage) increase accruing to the low-skilled. With sufficient complementarity between the low and high-skilled workers, the low-skilled subsidize to some extent the education expenses of the medium-skilled. Johnson's analysis involves the explicit use of a production function in order to derive the gains made by the low-skilled workers as a result of having more of the highly skilled workers. The present approach, as mentioned in the previous chapter, does not specify a production function but instead simply imposes a relationship between the proportion of the population who invest in higher education and the productivity gains obtained by all individuals.

The present study develops a framework of analysis which allows for both the private and external benefits of education, treated as an investment rather than a consumption good. The revenue implications of any subsidy scheme are dealt with explicitly and education involves forgone earnings in view of the time required to gain skills. A continuous distribution of ability is used, rather than the discrete form used by Johnson.

Green and Sheshinski (1975) analysed the implications of the government funding of higher education, where a positive externality is generated, under the assumption that the government maximizes a utilitarian social welfare function. They took the total amount available for higher education funding as exogenous and found that increases in this given amount lead to a more regressive distribution of government funds. Furthermore, an increase in the size of the externality generated by higher education also leads to a more regressive distribution. The major contrast between their analysis and the present study is that Green and Sheshinski give no consideration to the financing of the education subsidy. The model developed below analyses the revenue requirement of the government and thus is also able to model the precise choice of the amount of funding in the light of the government's budget constraint. Despite these differences, it will be found that the inclusion of a revenue constraint reinforces Green and Sheshinski's (1975) study. A comparison of marginal costs and benefits of increasing the level of the tax-financed grant shows that regressive higher education funding increases with an increase in externalities generated by higher education.

Mention may also be made of the approach taken by Ulph (1977). He found that, in order to maximize total income for a given level of inequality aversion, progressivity in the tax and transfer system is complemented by regressivity in the distribution of education subsidies. Ulph modelled the disincentive of high marginal tax rates and found that if society's distributional objectives are achieved through the tax system then the consequent loss in income can be redressed by increasing the subsidy to higher education. Although Ulph's (1977) consideration of aspects of the progressivity of the tax system is an attempt to draw connections between state funding of higher education and the tax system, he did not model the government's budget constraint. Furthermore Ulph did not consider the effects of taxes and higher education subsidies on individuals' investment decisions, nor the implications of an externality generated by higher education. However, the following analysis, which allows for these extra interdependencies and the externalities, also reinforces Ulph's results. A rise in the progressivity of the tax system leads to a decline in the incentive to invest in higher education, so education enrolments fall. However, the dependence of the external benefits generated by higher education on the proportion educated implies that it becomes more profitable for the government to finance higher education through the tax system, irrespective of its decision-making objective. Thus, as found by Ulph, higher education funding becomes more regressive.

2.2   EXTERNAL EFFECTS

The present study, as mentioned earlier, assumes that the external benefits from higher education, in the form of general productivity gains, are related to the proportion of the population that invests in higher education. An immediate difficulty is that, despite the huge literature on the external benefits of education (and higher education as just one component), no attempt has been made to estimate such a relationship. The majority of studies fall into the 'growth accounting' framework, involving the interpretation of a 'residual', after allowing for the growth of input of factors of production. This literature is far too extensive to discuss here, and a more detailed examination is not really warranted in view of its minor contribution to the present study. Detailed reviews can be found in, for example, Hope and Miller (1988) and Leslie and Brinkman (1988).

In Denison (1984), the proportion of growth in net national income not explained by increases in the productivity of land and capital is attributed to increases in labour productivity and miscellaneous causes. Of this, a proportion is attributed to education, of which a further proportion is attributed to higher education. Denison separates the data into two periods: 1948–73 and 1973–81. For the first period he takes the total annual percentage growth rate of 3.59 and attributes 1.6 to advances in land and capital, with the remaining 1.99 to advances in knowledge and miscellaneous determinants. He finds that advancement in knowledge forms 71 per cent of this residual and therefore 40 per cent of total growth. Results are similar for the later period. On the argument that tertiary education contributes to approximately one-quarter of this, Denison's results suggest that tertiary education adds roughly one-third of a percentage point to the growth rate per year. Others have obtained comparable results, including Schultz (1963, 1981), Psacharopoulos (1973), Jorgenson (1984), Kendrick (1983) and McMahon (1984).

There has of course been considerable criticism of this approach, particularly the assumption that a correlation between education and growth is proof of causation and the attribution of such a large proportion of knowledge advancement to education. Chinloy (1980) argues that the contribution of education cannot be considered in isolation since much of this would not have come about without concomitant changes in other social and economic variables. However, Psacharopoulos (1984) argues that in part these comcomitant changes are in fact caused by education. He also argues that earlier studies do not account for the increasing labour force which requires greater educational expense just to maintain standards. Thus Psacharopoulos gives a figure much higher than that of Denison.

It must be recognized that all the studies have a degree of arbitrariness in determining the exact magnitude of growth effects and even more arbitrariness is introduced when calculating the contribution of a particular component of education, as in the tertiary contribution relevant here. In view of this difficulty, it is particularly important to carry out sensitivity analyses rather than rely on a particular set of estimates.

2.3   INCOME INEQUALITY

It was suggested in Chapter 1 that a standard normative argument for the use of tax-financed subsidies, that they can contribute towards egalitarian income redistribution, cannot apply in the present context. Rather, the appropriate question, raised by several authors, is why subsidies should be given when they are inherently regressive. Nevertheless, there has been much debate on the redistributive effect of subsidies for higher education. It is argued here that a major reason why this important question remains unresolved is due to the lack of a model which can deal with the many interdependencies. Partial approaches have previously been applied, often leading to the inconsistent treatment of crucial features. This section begins by isolating several basic issues involved in any study of redistribution, and examines previous studies with respect to their treatment of these areas. It emerges that most previous studies of the redistributive effects of higher education grants use a static or annual approach. However, it is argued that a lifetime approach is necessary since both the costs and benefits of higher education grants are borne over the entire working life.

Approaches to Budgetary Incidence

Analyses of the incidence of government expenditure use several different approaches. It is useful, following De Wulf (1981), to distinguish four broad categories: The 'money flow' approach, the 'on whose behalf are expenditures made' approach, the 'expenditure incidence' approach and the 'benefit incidence' approach. These approaches differ in the degree to which they consider the general equilibrium implications of government expenditure.

The money flow approach follows a simple accounting framework. The beneficiaries of government expenditure on education are taken as being the teachers who receive payment for their services. It would seem more sensible, however, to attribute some benefit to those receiving the subsidized education, which is the essence of the 'on whose behalf are expenditures made' approach. De Wulf suggests that most studies of budgetary incidence fall into this category, though it takes no account of general equilibrium effects. In the present context, the main shortcomings of this second approach are that it ignores the enhanced earning capacity of those induced to invest in higher education as a result of a subsidy, changes in tax rates and any externalities generated by education.

An important limitation is that authors rarely specify a counterfactual situation. In general the difficulty involved in establishing a suitable counterfactual varies with the size of government expenditure being examined. In the extreme, analysis of the incidence of total government expenditure would require a simulation of the whole economy in the absence not only of government expenditure, but also the laws and regulations sanctioned by government. It is less difficult to establish a counterfactual for the provision of higher education grants. Those who have attempted this are categorized as supporting the 'expenditure incidence' approach. This requires that, as well as accounting for the direct beneficiaries, some regard is given to the effects on tax rates and factor prices. Higher grants would be expected to increase tax rates and perhaps also reduce the earnings of graduates.

Finally, the 'benefit incidence' approach values government expenditure in terms of the benefit to recipients rather than the cost of provision. Thus De Wulf (1981, p. 61) argues that the benefit of grants should be related to the present value of the increase in net earnings of recipients. A complete examination also needs to account for any externality stemming from higher education, and to determine if the benefits bear some relation to the cost of providing the good. Furthermore, it is important, as also argued by Greene (1973), that in measuring benefits attention should be given to the method of government decision-making.

Although most studies have worked within the 'on whose behalf are expenditures made' approach, there exist significant distinctions between authors over their approach to some basic issues. These differences are discussed below and explain some of the divergence in results obtained. Some authors have also attempted to extend the analysis by tackling the general equilibrium aspects. Examining these attempts will not only help to explain the differences between authors but will suggest more suitable methods to be used in further analysis.

It is important in examining income redistribution to be clear about the treatment of the following issues. First, a decision must be made about the time period of analysis. Secondly, the income unit must also be specified and this will often be linked to the decision on the time period. Thirdly, it is necessary to consider any externalities generated by the expenditure. Fourthly, changes in eligibility for benefits and the way in which this is altered by changes in the level of spending needs to be taken into account. Finally, an appropriate counterfactual must be specified. Previous studies can therefore usefully be distinguished according to their treatment of these aspects. A brief summary of some studies is given in Table 2.1, which shows immediately not only how they differ, but that some studies are internally inconsistent.

Table 2.1   *Tax incidence studies*

Author	Time period Grant	Tax	Income unit		Education response	External effects	Counter factual
Hansen and Weisbrod (1969a)	A	L	X	F	n.a.	n.a.	No
Hansen and Weisbrod (1969b)	A	L	X	F	n.a.	Extra product	No
Pechman (1970)	A	A	X	F	n.a.	n.a.	No
Crean (1975)	L	A	C	F	n.a.	n.a.	No
Conlisk (1977)	L	L	X	I	Response parameter	n.a.	Yes
McGuire (1976)	L	A	C	F	n.a.	n.a.	No
Shackett and Slottje (1987)	Time series		X	I	Reflected through incomes	All possible effects	No
James and Benjamin (1988a)	L	L	C	F	n.a.	n.a.	No

Notes: L = Lifetime, A = Annual, X = Cross-section, C = Cohort, F = Family, I = Individual, n.a. = not applicable.

The Time Period of Analysis

Contributions to costs of subsidies through tax payments occur over the working life of educated and non-educated persons. Benefits generally accrue over time as a result of increased future earning potential. Those authors in Table 2.1 who use an annual approach ignore increased earnings and the partial deferred payment of fees via taxation after higher education. Several authors recognize that the benefits vary over an individual's lifetime, but they nevertheless take a rather partial approach. For example, some authors have attempted to allow for lifecycle effects by arguing that income units should only be compared at similar points in the lifecycle. Crean (1975) argues for a comparison of benefits and contributions only within cohorts of equivalently aged children. McGuire (1976) limits his analysis to a cohort of families where the family head is between 39 and 60 years of age, but ignores tax contributions. James and Benjamin (1988a) consider the aggregate income distribution but adjust the incomes of families which may have children of university age. This requires the assumption that the distribution of income remains relatively constant through time. In listing the proportion of units receiving subsidies, within an income group, these authors exclude individuals who are ineligible for benefits in view of their age. They find that, after allowing for this factor, those in the lower percentiles of the population are more highly represented among the beneficiaries of subsidies.

Hansen and Weisbrod (1969a) and Pechman (1970) compare benefits received in terms of annual data, recording tuition subsidies for all income units irrespective of their age. However, Pechman (1970) does not advocate such an approach and emphasizes the lifetime nature of redistribution. His purpose in using this approach is to demonstrate that, even with the same data as used by Hansen and Weisbrod (1969a), different results will be obtained when comparisons are made between different groups. Those units who are, due to their age, ineligible to receive benefits are counted as not receiving a benefit in the same way as are individuals who are of an eligible age but do not, for whatever reason, receive benefits. This is clearly an inferior approach as it must mistakenly attribute some variability in benefits received to differences in wealth instead of differences in age.

Most authors do not allow for the enhanced earnings of the educated, which is probably the major benefit. Crean (1975) and McGuire (1976) restrict their analyses to annual data, listing both the direct benefits received within the specified age groups and the taxes paid over that period. James and Benjamin (1988a) are more ambitious, assuming that, within a cohort, individual relative incomes remain constant. They track age groups through time and calculate both the direct educational receipts and lifetime tax payments of families within each group. They extrapolate from a cross-sectional income distribution to a lifetime income distribution by assuming that relative incomes within a cohort do not vary. But this is unjustified because the dispersion of access to education in part determines the nature of this distribution and it is well established that the dispersion of earnings varies with age. Conlisk (1977, p. 154) also argues that the way in which earnings are altered by the subsidy needs to be taken into account.

Hansen and Weisbrod (1969b. p. 56) attempt to calculate the extra tax payments of the educated over time by estimating the lifetime tax payments of the arithmetic mean educated individual. But this is not, in general, the approach most favoured by them. It represents an attempt to incorporate a lifetime approach, but leads to internal inconsistency as they allow the increased earnings of the educated to affect their lifetime tax payments but take no account of the extra earnings of the educated which contribute to the lifetime benefit.

The Income Unit

In the choice of income unit, the major distinction is between the family and the individual. Hansen and Weisbrod (1969a, 1969b) and Pechman (1970) consider a cross-section of families, while Conlisk (1977) considers a cross-section of individuals where earning potential and the likelihood of investing in higher education are related to parental characteristics. Shackett and Slottje (1987) consider data on individual incomes, using a time series of cross-sections.

There is, however, an advantage in limiting the analysis of lifecycle effects to a single cohort of individuals. This is not to deny that a component of the lifetime redistribution is between cohorts, but merely makes explicit the distinction between intra- and inter-cohort effects. In general, a within-cohort lifetime analysis cannot be undertaken for a comparison between families, as a family is composed of individuals from different cohorts. However, Crean (1975), McGuire (1976) and James and Benjamin (1988a) all apply a within-cohort family analysis by ranking families according to the age of the family head. McGuire (1976) considers parental income for parents aged between 39 and 60 without allowing for some students being financially or legally independent of their parents. Crean (1975) and James and Benjamin (1988a) similarly consider family income for each cohort, although over a wider range of cohorts than considered by Crean (1975). This approach may be justified in an annual framework, but in a lifetime context the problems raised by families being composed of individuals of different ages cannot be overcome by focusing on the head of the family. Through time, the composition of the family unit changes along with the distribution of income within the family.

External Effects

Those operating within the 'on whose behalf are expenditures made' approach have not in general considered externalities, as they have taken an annual approach and the external effects of higher education would be expected to operate through time. However, a more comprehensive approach requires that some account be taken of the externalities generated by higher education. Few authors have attempted to estimate these effects, possibly due to their illusiveness. Hansen and Weisbrod (1969b) make some attempt by incorporating the extra productivity of the educated through their working life but find this to be inconsequential. However, even if productivity increases had been significant they do not represent an externality unless it is demonstrated that they are not fully reflected in higher wages to the educated. Conlisk (1977) accounts for extra taxes paid by the educated through their enhanced earning potential but includes no provision for any external effects. Shackett and Slottje (1987) analyse a time series of incomes with higher education used as one of the explanatory variables. Even though education is found to have a significant effect on inequality, it is not clear whether the effects are a consequence of external economies or direct benefits in the form of grants.

Given the uncertainty surrounding the size and nature of externalities generated by higher education it would seem best to compare the results obtained using differing assumptions about externalities. If measured inequality is found to be sensitive to the assumed size and nature of these externalities then this should be made explicit. Haveman and Wolfe (1984) also provide an extensive review of previous estimates of external, non-monetary benefits generated by education.

Endogenous Educational Choice

Most authors assume that educational choice is not responsive to changes in subsidies. Since the educated are largely from the upper tail of the income distribution, subsidies represent a distribution towards those members of the population who may anyway have chosen to become educated. However, it is likely that there are some individuals who, without subsidies, find the costs too high in relation to the benefits and, even where capital markets are perfect, will not invest in education. Conlisk (1977) attempts to account for these individuals, but does this in a rather *ad hoc* way by including a parameter which can vary with the income background of students. Conlisk (1977, p. 153) emphasizes the ambiguity of changes in tuition subsidy on inequality. However, it seems from his discussion that much of the ambiguity stems from the response of previously uneducated individuals. This response can be more fully analysed when educational decisions are considered in a lifetime context.

The Counterfactual Situation

Finally, it is important to establish a well-defined counterfactual situation. With the direct 'on whose behalf are expenditures made' approach, the counterfactual is simply the situation that would occur had the benefits not been paid and is obtained by subtracting the value of the benefit from those who received it. However, as discussed above, the existence of benefits has many indirect effects which cannot be ignored.

It has already been noted that most authors listed in Table 2.1 consider only the direct changes in tuition costs and their immediate extra tax burden. Only Conlisk (1977) considers the interaction of individuals' education decisions with the government's provision of tuition grants, subject to a budget constraint. A further interdependency is the effect which individual actions have on the level of funding chosen by the government. James and Benjamin (1988b) consider government subsidies as the endogenous outcome of political processes. In their analysis, the Japanese system of funding for higher education is explained in terms of the behaviour of vote-maximizing political agents. A similar approach can be usefully applied to analyse the level of government grant for education where the inequality effects of such grants are the focus of investigation. Further analysis of inequality is given in Chapter 7.

3.   A general framework of analysis

This chapter examines the value of a higher education grant, financed from income taxation, which a majority of the members of a cohort will support even though members of that majority do not themselves invest in higher education. A general equilibrium approach is taken that allows for important interdependencies between the proportion of the population educated, the tax rate required to finance grants, and external benefits of higher education. These interdependencies imply that the determinants of majority support and the characterization of an equilibrium preferred level of grant is rather complex. The first chapter examined these issues in a non-technical way using only diagrams, and it was found that although some important interdependencies could usefully be illustrated, qualitative results were quite limited. The present chapter thus represents an attempt to examine the interdependencies and the nature of the majority voting equilibrium in more detail. However, specific functional forms are in most cases avoided at this stage. Section 3.1 provides a statement of the formal framework which incorporates the relevant interdependencies. Section 3.2 uses the framework to characterize an equilibrium preferred level of a grant, and section 3.3 analyses the comparative static properties of the model. In particular, the effects on the preferred level of the grant of changes in the private returns to education, the amount of external benefit generated by higher education and the level of government non-education expenditure are examined.

Abstracting, for the moment, from the difficulty involved in finding an equilibrium, it is necessary to consider the factors which determine an individual's support for tax-financed higher education grants. These were examined in Chapter 1 and are therefore discussed only briefly in the present chapter, although a little repetition is unavoidable. If grants are financed through the income tax system, they impose a cost through higher tax rates but may also provide benefits if higher education generates an externality. The amount of the extra tax burden depends upon the private returns to education, since the tax base rises with the proportion of the population educated, depending on the magnitude of these returns. Any externality which raises all incomes will also contribute to an increase in the tax base and will mitigate against increases in the tax burden.

The kind of external effect envisaged here is that of complementarity between skilled and unskilled workers in the production process. This has been modelled explicitly using a production function by Johnson (1984) and was discussed in Chapter 2. However, the present approach specifies the external effect in terms of the extent to which the earnings of all individuals are raised as a result of a proportion of the cohort investing in higher education. The externality is assumed to increase with the proportion of the population educated. Thus the increase in the externality caused by a given increase in the grant depends on the extent to which uneducated members of the cohort are induced to invest in higher education. However, the change in the proportion investing in higher education will itself depend upon the extent of the tax increase required to finance the increase in the grant which, as argued above, is itself determined by the magnitude of the private returns and the externality generated by higher education. The higher tax may be said to impose a deferred fee on the educated, paid over the working life following the period of higher education. Therefore tax rates, the proportion educated and the extent of the externality are jointly determined. In characterizing an equilibrium level of support for tax-financed higher education grants these interdependencies need to be considered explicitly within a general equilibrium model.

In order to examine an equilibrium (and assuming an interior solution to the first-order conditions), it is necessary to find a level of the grant at which marginal benefits and costs are equated for those individuals whose choice is decisive in determining the level of grant. This is made difficult by the fact that these costs and benefits are interdependent. Furthermore, a still greater degree of complexity is added when it is desired to analyse the comparative static properties of the model. This requires the analysis of changes in marginal costs and benefits, so that second-order conditions need to be examined explicitly. It will be found that qualitative analysis cannot always produce unambiguous results.

3.1 A COHORT MODEL

This section develops a more formal framework that can be used to analyse the interdependencies outlined above and in Chapter 1. The proportion of the direct fee or tuition cost of higher education which is financed by taxation is denoted by ρ. The value of ρ that an uneducated majority of the cohort prefers is determined in a static general equilibrium model. Since higher education is treated as an investment, it is necessary to take a lifetime approach.

The Determination of Net Lifetime Income

Assume that each individual's pre-tax income is determined by income-earning ability, y. The analysis abstracts from variations in labour supply, which may otherwise be induced by differences in ability, preferences and the income tax structure. Individuals range from low to high ability where the distribution function is given by $F(y)$. Suppose that the tax system is proportional so that tax at the rate t is levied on all income. The general growth of incomes arising from the external benefit of education is denoted g; the nature of this benefit will be discussed in more detail later. The net lifetime income of an uneducated individual, for a given discount rate, may be written as:

$$V^N = V^N(t, y, g) \tag{3.1}$$

where V^N is assumed to be twice continuously differentiable, $V^N_t < 0$, $V^N_y > 0$, $V^N_g > 0$ and subscripts denote partial derivatives throughout.

The index of ability is chosen so that pre-tax income increases proportionately with ability. With the proportional tax system, this implies that V^N/y is equal for all uneducated individuals; in diagrammatic terms, the relationship between V^N and y is a straight line through the origin, as illustrated in Figure 3.1. Furthermore, $d(V^N/y)/dt$ is constant so that a change in t simply pivots the line about the origin. Assume also that each individual benefits from the external effects of education by an equal proportionate amount; hence $d(V^N/y)/dg$ is constant. This contrasts with the assumption in Johnson (1984) that differences in complementarity between the educated and uneducated, with just three skill levels, allow for different levels of external benefit.

Let c denote the direct cost of education, or fee, and u a parameter that determines the amount by which private earnings are raised through higher education. More specifically, it is assumed that the direct private proportional increase in earnings which results from investment in higher education is equal to uy. This implies that those with relatively high ability also receive a greater private benefit from higher education and thus have relatively steeper age–earnings profiles. Net lifetime income of an educated individual, V^E, can be written as:

$$V^E = V^E(t, u, c, \rho, y, g) \tag{3.2}$$

where V^E is assumed to be twice continuously differentiable, $V^E_t < 0$, $V^E_c < 0$, $V^E_\rho > 0$, $V^E_y > 0$, $V^E_g > 0$.

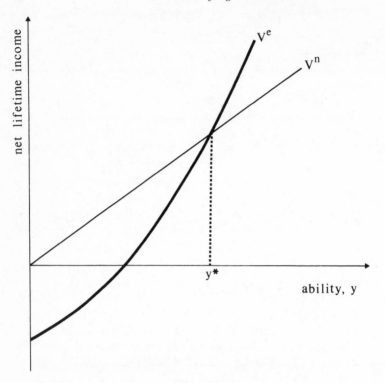

Figure 3.1   Net lifetime income and ability

The total cost of higher education for an individual includes not only the fixed cost, c, but also an opportunity cost which depends on ability, since it is necessary to forgo earnings during the period of higher education. The fixed fees are independent of ability, so $d(V^E/y)/dy > 0$. In diagrammatic terms, and as shown in Figure 3.1, the relationship between V^E and y gets steeper as y increases. It starts from below the horizontal axis because the costs outweigh the benefits of higher education for the low-ability individuals. Individuals of relatively higher income-earning ability gain relatively more through higher education. A further implication is that if the tuition cost of higher education is not tax-deductible, $d(V^E/y)/dt < d(V^N/y)/dt$.

Educational Choice

It is possible to find a level of ability, y^*, corresponding to that of an individual who is indifferent to investing in higher education, by setting $V^E = V^N$. The fixed cost component to education, and its corollary that V^E/y is rising in y, ensure that for all individuals with ability level $y > y^*$, net lifetime income is higher if educated. As shown in Figure 3.1, the V^E curve cuts the V^N line from below. Individuals are assumed to maximize net lifetime income. Thus the proportion of the population educated, p, corresponds to the proportion with ability above y^*. It is useful to refer to y^* as the *educational choice margin*. It is implicitly defined in terms of the factors that determine net lifetime income. The proportion of individuals with ability above y is given directly by $1 - F(y)$, so that p may be written as:

$$p = p(\rho, c, u, t) \tag{3.3}$$

where $p_\rho > 0$, $p_c < 0$, $p_u > 0$, $p_t < 0$. By the assumptions on V^E and V^N and since F is a distribution function, p is also twice differentiable. It is important to recognize that both V^N and V^E depend on the external effect measured by g, which depends on the proportion investing in higher education, p, which in turn depends on y^*. Hence the schedules illustrated in Figure 3.1 must be regarded as being fully consistent with the value of y^* given by their point of intersection.

For given ρ, c and u, (3.3) can also be viewed as giving a relationship between t and y^*. This takes the form shown in Figure 3.2, and may usefully be referred to as an *educational choice schedule*. As discussed in Chapter 1,

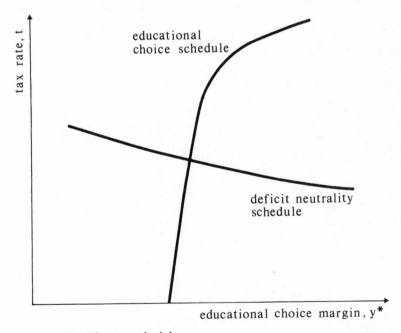

Figure 3.2   The two schedules

this schedule must be upward-sloping to the right. At low tax rates the choice margin is relatively insensitive to variations in t, but as the tax rate approaches unity, it is not worthwhile for anyone to invest in higher education.

The discount rate has not been included explicitly in the various functions used above. However, it may be noted that the private internal rate of return to higher education at the educational choice margin is equal to the discount rate. The extent to which the arithmetic mean rate of return, of those investing in higher education, exceeds the discount rate will depend partly on the form of the distribution function $F(y)$.

The second partial derivatives of the function in (3.3) are important in section 3.3 where comparative static results are examined. It is desirable to attach signs to these terms using only the assumptions made on V^N and V^E above. Since V^E/y is rising in y and V^N/y is constant, the educational choice margin, along with the proportion investing, $p = 1 - F(y^*)$, is determined by the intersection of a convex V^E and a linear V^N schedule, as shown in Figure 3.1. These schedules are useful in considering the second derivatives, by looking at the implications of the ways in which the two schedules change. The second derivatives of interest are $p_{\rho,u}, p_{t,u}, p_{\rho,t}, p_{t,t}$.

First, consider $p_{\rho,u}$, which reflects the way in which the responsiveness of the proportion investing, p, to the proportion of the fee that is given as a grant, ρ, changes as the private returns, u, increase. A change in both the private returns and the grant leave the V^N schedule in Figure 3.1 unchanged. However, an increase in the grant shifts the V^E schedule upwards by a constant amount, while an increase in the private returns makes this schedule steeper. Thus, for higher private returns (higher u), an increase in the grant (an increase in ρ) shifts upwards a steeper V^E schedule; this has a smaller effect on the educational choice margin than when private returns are lower and the schedule is flatter. It is therefore evident that $p_{\rho,u} < 0$. Secondly, consider $p_{\rho,t}$, which reflects the way in which the responsiveness of the proportion investing in higher education, p, to the tax-financed proportion of fees, ρ, changes when the tax rate changes. The increase in t must flatten both schedules in Figure 3.1 while, as suggested above, the increase in ρ shifts V^E upwards. But the reduction in the slope of the V^N schedule reduces the change in the educational choice margin due to an increase in the grant; hence the sign of $p_{\rho,t}$ is ambiguous. By a similar type of argument it can be shown that $p_{t,u}$ and $p_{t,t}$ are also ambiguous in sign.

The External Benefits of Education

The externality resulting from higher education is assumed to depend on p and an exogenous parameter, δ. For present purposes this may be regarded as a shift parameter. Hence write:

$$g = g(p, \delta) \tag{3.4}$$

where g is assumed to be twice continuously differentiable, with g_δ and $g_p > 0$. Consider the second derivatives of the external benefit function. Since the V^E schedule shown in Figure 3.1 is convex, it follows that the income-earning ability of the marginal individual falls as the proportion investing in higher education, p, increases, given the relationship between p and y^* given earlier. Thus if an educated individual's contribution to the externality generated by higher education is proportional to ability, the external growth function will be concave in p, so that $g_{p,p} < 0$. The shift parameter, δ, is defined so that $g_{p,\delta} > 0$, so that the slope of the relationship between g and p increases as δ increases. It might be suggested that the relationship between g and p would be expected to be convex for very small values of p, that is, when very few members of the cohort invest in higher education. Smyth (1991) argues that quality of higher education institutions is a marginally increasing function of resources over some ranges of expenditure. A similar argument could be made for the effect of p on g so that the function $g(p)$ would be sigmoid instead of concave. It is, however, assumed here that if $g(p)$ is sigmoid, p is large enough so that only the concave part of the function is relevant.

The Tax Base

Denote by z the arithmetic mean level of the present value of pre-tax income. For a given distribution of income-earning ability, the average lifetime income will depend on the proportion of the population educated and the private and social returns to higher education, so that in general z is a function of p, u and $g(p)$. It is most convenient to write this function simply as a function of p and u so that:

$$z = z(p, u) \tag{3.5}$$

where z is twice continuously differentiable and $z_p > 0$, $z_u > 0$. In considering the second derivatives, the convexity of the V^E schedule in Figure 3.1 is again important. An increase in the proportion investing in higher education, $p = 1 - F(y^*)$, implies that the additional people investing are of relatively lower ability, so that $z_{p,p} < 0$ and the relationship between z and p is concave. Furthermore, given the assumption that the proportional increase in earnings resulting from the private returns to higher education is itself proportional to the parameter u, it is clear that $z_{u,u} = 0$. Finally, the slope of relationship between average lifetime income and the proportion investing in higher education increases as the private returns increase, so that $z_{p,u} > 0$.

Government Deficit Neutrality

The proportional tax rate, t, must be set so that the total present value of tax revenue raised per member of the cohort is sufficient to finance both the government's grant towards the cost of higher education per person, given by ρpc, and an exogenous amount of government non-education expenditure per person, in present value terms given by R, to be financed through the income tax system. Total expenditure per person is thus equal to $R + \rho pc$, and the deficit neutrality condition for the cohort requires that this must equal the present value of the tax revenue raised from the proportional income tax system, given by tz. This condition is not as straightforward as it may initially appear to be, since the terms p and z themselves depend on t. Hence the deficit neutrality condition is highly non-linear, but the required value of t can be implicitly defined by:

$$t = t(\rho, c, p, R, z) \tag{3.6}$$

where $t_p > 0, t_c > 0, t_R > 0, t_z < 0$. From the differentiability of z and p, t is also twice continuously differentiable. The budget constraint may also be viewed in terms of a schedule relating t to y^*, for fixed values of the other parameters. This is referred to as a *deficit neutrality schedule*, and it takes the form shown in Figure 3.2.

In principle, the derivative t_p is ambiguous in sign because, if the contribution of the additional higher-educated people to the tax base is large enough and/or if ρ is low, then it is possible that t can fall with an increase in p. However, it may be expected that a rise in p raises t, as the cost of financing the grant of the additional members of the cohort who invest in higher education outweighs their positive contribution to the tax base. If this were not the case, higher education outlays would increase the government's revenue and it would follow trivially that uneducated individuals would favour funding of higher education. Psacharopoulos and Woodhall (1985) look directly at the effect of government-induced increases in education on net government revenue (which they call the fiscal rate of return) and find that it is negative. It is assumed that the non-education government expenditure has no effect on individual's income earning ability.

The second derivatives of interest are $t_{p,R}$, $t_{p,R}$, $t_{p,z}$ and $t_{p,p}$. The term $t_{p,R}$ equals zero because the effect of an increase in ρ on the proportional tax rate is independent of the level of government non-education expenditure; similarly $t_{p,R} = 0$. Furthermore, $t_{p,z} < 0$ as a higher tax base mitigates the effect of a given increase in ρ on the proportional tax rate. Conversely $t_{p,p} > 0$ as total government expenditure for a given ρ rises with p.

3.2   MAJORITY VOTING

The Majority Voting Equilibrium

Individuals are assumed to vote over the proportion of the costs of higher education, ρ, that they wish to see financed by taxation. Hence choice concerns the single variable ρ rather than joint decision-taking over a combination of R and ρ. It is well known that voting over more than one variable can lead to serious problems. Furthermore, as argued in Chapter 1, it is not entirely unrealistic to consider the government as taking a more partial approach to various issues, despite the general attraction in principle of a more comprehensive view. To an uneducated individual, financing a proportion of the fee through ρ imposes a tax cost reflected in a higher tax rate, t, and a benefit through the external effect determined by g. The effect of ρ on both t and g has been shown to be complex and in Chapter 1 it was suggested that some individuals will be expected to have double-peaked preferences over the size of the higher education grant. However, it is shown here that, from the assumptions made above on V^N, a majority voting equilibrium exists, even though preferences may not be single-peaked.

It is a standard result that double-peaked preferences can give rise to cyclical voting, and in the present context there are likely to be some individuals who prefer to see ρ fall over a range, when they do not themselves invest in higher education, but then prefer to see ρ increased after it passes a level which induces them to invest. Figure 3.3 illustrates the situation for three types of individual. The lower schedule applies to those who never become educated, even for high values of ρ. The top schedule applies to individuals who always invest in higher education whether or not there is a grant; even for them there is a finite limit to the preferred grant because of the tax implications. The middle schedule describes the preferences of an individual who is induced to invest as ρ reaches a critical value.

An uneducated individual would select the value of ρ which maximizes V^N given by (3.1). The first-order condition for this maximization implies that for a given level of income-earning ability, y:

$$-(\mathrm{d}V^N/\mathrm{d}g)(\mathrm{d}g/\mathrm{d}\rho) = (\mathrm{d}t/\mathrm{d}\rho)(\mathrm{d}V^N/\mathrm{d}t). \tag{3.7}$$

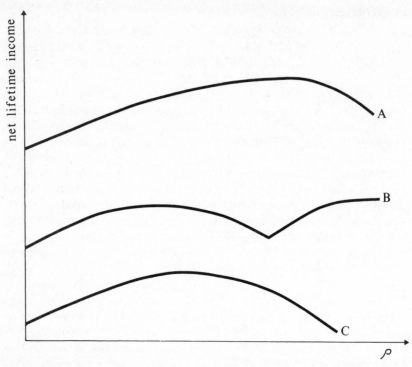

Figure 3.3   Variations in net lifetime income

This result simply states that the marginal benefit of an increase in ρ (through the external effect, g) and the marginal cost (through the tax rate, t) are equal. The analysis ignores a possible supply constraint facing students by assuming an interior solution to the first-order condition. The existence of a binding supply constraint implies that $\partial p/\partial \rho = 0$, and therefore $\partial g/\partial \rho = 0$, so that an upper limit would be imposed on ρ, as discussed in section 1.2 of Chapter 1. The following analysis concentrates on interior solutions.

Since all pre-tax income is taxed proportionately and earnings resulting from the externality are proportional to income-earning ability, the first-order condition (3.7) is independent of y. Since V^N represents the net lifetime income of an individual with $y < y^*$, all individuals below the educational choice margin are therefore unanimous in their support for a particular value of ρ. It is realistic to assume that a majority of the cohort does not invest in higher education, so that $F(y^*) > 0.5$, and the value of ρ which maximizes V^N for any (and thus all) $y < y^*$ is a majority voting equilibrium.

Formal Statement of the Solution

Equations (3.1)–(3.7) describe a general equilibrium model with endogenous variables g, p, t, z and ρ (along with the net lifetime income of each member of the cohort) and exogenous variables c, u, R, δ and the distribution function $F(y)$. If most people are uneducated, a majority of the cohort will unanimously choose that level of ρ which maximizes their net lifetime income. Of relevance are the effect of the grant on the proportion investing in higher education, given by (3.3), and in turn the latter's effect on the external benefit and the tax base, through (3.4) and (3.5) respectively. These benefits, which arise through the ρ's effect on the tax base, z, and the proportion investing, p, as well as an indirect effect through the external benefit, g, will be contrasted with the costs of the grant, which affect net lifetime income, V^N, through the tax rate, t. The value of t must satisfy (3.6). Formally, the majority voting equilibrium can be stated as:

$$\max_{\rho} \ V^N(g[p\{\rho\}, \delta], t[p\{\rho\}, z\{p(\rho), u, \rho\}]). \tag{3.8}$$

Equation (3.2) is not considered explicitly because the preferences of those investing in higher education do not have any effect on the majority voting outcome; however, it does enter implicitly in the determination of p through (3.3). By the continuity of V^N in ρ and by the maximum theorem a solution to (3.8) exists. As noted above, some of those who invest in higher education are likely to have double-peaked preferences; for relatively low values of ρ they prefer the grant to fall as they are below the educational choice margin, y^*, but as ρ increases beyond a critical value they become educated and prefer it to increase even more. Furthermore, some very high-ability individuals may prefer the grant to be very low or even zero, because otherwise they have to pay a high 'deferred fee' in the form of *extra* tax payments which exceed the value of the grant.

The first-order condition in equation (3.7), which is necessary for the maximization of net lifetime income for an uneducated individual, can be written more fully as:

$$\frac{\partial V}{\partial g} \frac{\partial g}{\partial p} \left\{ \frac{\partial p}{\partial \rho} + \frac{\partial p}{\partial t} \frac{\partial t}{\partial \rho} \right\} + \frac{\partial V}{\partial t} \left\{ \frac{\partial t}{\partial \rho} + \frac{\partial t}{\partial p} \frac{\partial p}{\partial \rho} + \frac{\partial t}{\partial z} \frac{\partial z}{\partial p} \frac{\partial p}{\partial \rho} \right\} = 0 \tag{3.9}$$

where the superscript has been omitted from V for convenience. It will be assumed below that the second-order condition for a maximum is satisfied, so that the second-order term, denoted [SOT], is less than zero. Equation (3.9) is in general rather complex, but it implicitly defines a function $\rho^*(.)$ which relates the preferred level of ρ to the exogenous parameters. By the maximum theorem, ρ^* is also a continuous function. If the function $\rho^*(.)$ is substituted for ρ in equation (3.9) this yields the following identity:

$$\frac{\partial V}{\partial g}\frac{\partial g}{\partial p}\left\{\frac{\partial p}{\partial \rho^*(.)}+\frac{\partial p}{\partial t}\frac{\partial t}{\partial \rho^*(.)}\right\}+\frac{\partial V}{\partial t}\left\{\frac{\partial t}{\partial \rho^*(.)}+\frac{\partial t}{\partial p}\frac{dp}{\partial \rho^*(.)}+\frac{\partial t}{\partial z}\frac{\partial z}{\partial p}\frac{\partial p}{\partial \rho^*(.)}\right\}=0.$$

$$(3.10)$$

It is possible to take the derivative of (3.10) with respect to changes in exogenous parameters in order to determine the effect of these changes on the optimal value, ρ^*. Several comparative static exercises of this kind are considered in the next section. These more formal analyses may be compared with the discussion in Chapter 1 which investigates how far the argument can be taken by simply shifting the deficit neutrality and educational choice schedules, such as those in Figure 3.2.

3.3   SOME COMPARATIVE STATICS

An Increase in Non-education Expenditure

It might perhaps be thought that an increase in other government expenditure, R, which requires a higher tax rate, would reduce the willingness of the majority of the cohort to have tax-financed grants. However, when further interdependencies are considered, it is seen that the story is much more complicated. Taking the derivative of (3.10) with respect to R, and rearranging, yields an expression for $d\rho^*/dR$. This is a very complex expression, but the form of the deficit neutrality function, in equation (3.6), allows some simplification. It was seen above that both $t_{\rho,R}$ and $t_{p,R}$ are zero, so that a *ceteris paribus* change in R does not affect the marginal effect of a rise in ρ or p on the tax rate. Thus the derivative of (3.10) with respect to R simplifies to:

$$[\text{SOT}]\ \frac{d\rho^*}{dR}=-\overset{+}{\frac{\partial V}{\partial g}}\left\{\overset{+}{\frac{\partial p}{\partial \rho}}+\overset{-}{\frac{\partial p}{\partial t}}\overset{+}{\frac{\partial t}{\partial \rho}}\right\}\overset{-}{\frac{\partial^2 g}{\partial p^2}}\overset{-}{\frac{\partial p}{\partial t}}\overset{+}{\frac{\partial t}{\partial R}}$$

$$-\overset{+}{\frac{\partial V}{\partial g}}\overset{+}{\frac{\partial g}{\partial p}}\left\{\overset{+}{\frac{\partial^2 p}{\partial \rho \partial t}}\overset{+}{\frac{\partial t}{\partial R}}\overset{+}{\frac{\partial t}{\partial \rho}}+\overset{+}{\frac{\partial^2 p}{\partial t^2}}\overset{+}{\frac{\partial t}{\partial R}}\overset{+}{\frac{\partial t}{\partial \rho}}\right\}$$

$$-\overset{-}{\frac{\partial V}{\partial t}}\overset{+}{\frac{\partial^2 p}{\partial \rho \partial t}}\overset{+}{\frac{\partial t}{\partial R}}\left\{\overset{-}{\frac{\partial t}{\partial p}}+\overset{+}{\frac{\partial t}{\partial z}}\frac{\partial z}{\partial p}\right\}-\overset{-}{\frac{\partial V}{\partial t}}\overset{-}{\frac{\partial t}{\partial z}}\overset{-}{\frac{\partial^2 z}{\partial p^2}}\overset{-}{\frac{\partial p}{\partial t}}\overset{+}{\frac{\partial p}{\partial \rho}}\overset{+}{\frac{\partial t}{\partial R}}$$

$$-\frac{\overset{-}{\partial V}}{\partial t}\frac{\overset{-}{\partial^2 t}}{\partial z \partial R}\frac{\overset{+}{\partial z}}{\partial p}\frac{\overset{+}{\partial p}}{\partial \rho}. \tag{3.11}$$

The sign of each component is shown above it, except where the earlier discussion has shown that the sign is ambiguous. The first term in (3.11) depends upon the sign of $\partial p/\partial \rho + (\partial p/\partial t)(\partial t/\partial \rho)$, which measures the net effect of a change in ρ on the proportion investing in higher education, p. This is positive as the direct effect, $\partial p/\partial \rho$, is greater than the induced fall in p due to the increased tax rate resulting from a higher grant, $(\partial p/\partial t)(\partial t/\partial \rho)$. The sign of the first term follows from the concavity of the growth function with respect to p. If R rises, the proportion investing falls and an increase in the grant, which induces an increase in p, has a greater marginal external benefit.

The fourth and fifth terms are also positive. The sign of the fourth term follows from the concavity of the tax base with respect to the proportion investing in higher education, since a rise in p implies that the marginal person is of relatively lower income-earning ability. A rise in R which leads to a rise in the tax rate and thus a fall in the proportion investing implies that, in order to support a given increase in the grant, the tax rate needs to rise by relatively less; this is because the tax base effect of increased p on the arithmetic mean lifetime income, induced through the rise in the grant, is larger. The fifth term shows that an uneducated person will benefit from an increasing tax base generated through a rise in the grant, and therefore the proportion investing, by a greater amount when R is high. This is because the tax rate is initially high, so the rise in the grant mitigates some of the effect of the rise in the tax rate due to the rise in other government expenditure, R.

The second and third terms are ambiguous as $p_{\rho,t}$ and $p_{t,t}$ are ambiguous in sign. However, it can be argued that these ambiguous terms are relatively small. In section 3.2 it was argued that $p_{\rho,t}$ is either zero or small and negative, and t_p is positive. Thus if $p_{\rho,t}$ is negative the third term is positive. This shows that with a higher R and a consequently higher tax rate there is a smaller effect of ρ on the proportion investing and therefore a smaller effect of ρ on t; thus ρ^* rises. It may however be expected that the effect of this term is minor compared with the previous terms, as $p_{\rho,t}$ will be small over a reasonable range of the tax rate.

Finally, the second term also depends upon $p_{\rho,t}$ and another ambiguous term $p_{t,t}$. This term captures how the effect of the grant on the proportion investing changes with a change in the tax rate which is induced by an increase in other government expenditure, R. The increase in the grant increases the proportion investing through its direct effect and also acts to lower it through its increase in the tax rate; however, as argued earlier, the direct effect will dominate so that the proportion investing increases. The second term captures how the two effects of ρ and p change with the level of t; however, since $p_{\rho,t}$ and $p_{t,t}$ are ambiguous it is impossible to determine its sign. But, even if it were negative, it would be small in comparison to the four other positive terms as both $p_{\rho,t}$ and $p_{t,t}$ are small over a reasonable range of t. Hence, although $d\rho^*/\partial R$ is not unambiguously positive in sign, there is a strong presumption that $d\rho^*/dR > 0$. Interestingly, this result is similar to that found by Bös (1980) where a markedly different majority voting model is used.

An Increase in the External Effect of Education

The effect of an increase in the externality, resulting from an increase in the parameter δ, is more straightforward. Following a similar process, the derivative of (3.10) with respect to δ yields:

$$[SOT] \quad \frac{d\rho^*}{d\delta} = - \frac{\overset{+}{\partial^2 g}}{\partial p \partial \delta} \left\{ \overset{+}{\frac{\partial p}{\partial \rho}} + \overset{-}{\frac{\partial p}{\partial t}} \overset{+}{\frac{\partial t}{\partial \rho}} \right\}$$

By the same reasoning as that used above, the term in brackets must be positive. The direct effect of an increase in the grant on the proportion investing exceeds the indirect effect caused by the increase in the tax rate; therefore an increase in the external effect via δ leads unambiguously to a rise in the majority choice of higher education grant. An increase in δ implies that when the higher grant induces a rise in the proportion investing in higher education, it contributes more to the external effect, and thus makes all individuals better off. Unlike the result of the previous subsection, this result is intuitively easy to accept.

An Increase in the Private Benefits of Education

The private benefits of education, reflected in the parameter u, affect the proportion investing and the tax rate directly as well as indirectly through the external effect and the tax base. Therefore it is not surprising to find that $d\rho^*/du$ is ambiguous in sign. Taking the derivative of (3.10) with respect to u yields an expression that is too lengthy to be usefully reproduced here. However, it is instructive to consider some of the effects. Higher u leads to a higher proportion investing and, since the external effect g is concave in p, funding-induced rises in p yield lower benefits; thus downward pressure is exerted on ρ^*. Also, changes in the tax rate induced by a change in the tax base fall with u. This is because a higher u is associated with a high proportion investing and, as there is a higher fixed spending component, the tax base is also higher. The effect of a change in the tax base on lowering the tax rate is smaller if the base is initially high; thus there is further downward pressure on ρ^*. Conversely since $p_{\rho,u} < 0$, there is upward pressure on the optimal value ρ^*. Here, increasing the grant leads to a smaller increase in the proportion investing, so that changes in ρ require less revenue and in turn imply less upward pressure on the tax rate. Considering only these effects demonstrates the impossibility of attaching a sign to this comparative static result and again suggests the need for a model with more structure. Such a model is examined in the following chapter.

4.   Majority voting with a proportional income tax

It was seen in the previous chapter that only limited qualitative results can be obtained using a general framework of analysis designed to handle some of the major interdependencies of interest. This chapter adds more structure to the model, in order to specify the precise nature of the educational choice and deficit neutrality schedules, and thereby obtain quantitative orders of magnitude. The basic framework is the same. It is a two-period cohort model in which individuals either work or invest in higher education in the first period, and all individuals work in the second period. Income in the first period, if the individual works, is denoted by $y_i (i = 1, \ldots, N)$. This is determined by the individual's endowment of ability which affects both income in the first period and the ability to benefit from higher education, in that those with a higher value of y obtain a higher private rate of return from education. The endowment may be regarded as depending on ability and family background; the precise transformation of these factors to produce y need not be considered explicitly for present purposes.

Education involves an opportunity cost, such that a proportion, $1 - h$, of y is forgone by each individual undergoing higher education. The cost of education per person is denoted c, of which only a proportion, $(1 - \rho)$, is borne by the individual. The remainder, ρc, is given as an unconditional grant and is financed from income taxation. For an individual who has invested in higher education, income in the second period is higher than that in the first period by a proportion s_i. However, higher education is also assumed to raise the earnings of all individuals by the rate, g, through a general increase in productivity. The precise amount depends on the proportion, p, of the cohort that invests in higher education, so that $g = g(p)$.

This chapter concentrates on the use of majority voting in the context of a proportional income tax. Section 4.1 derives the educational choice schedule, while section 4.2 obtains the form of the deficit neutrality schedule, which is complicated by the need to derive an explicit expression for the total (present value of) lifetime income in the cohort. The iterative procedure used to solve the non-linear model is described in section 4.3, and is followed by a selection of numerical examples which throw further light on the comparative static properties of the model.

4.1 EDUCATIONAL CHOICE OF INDIVIDUALS

It is first necessary to determine which individuals will become educated, for given values of the parameters of the model. As in the previous chapter, it is assumed that the supply of education is demand-determined. Suppose that the income tax system involves a simple proportional rate of tax, t, on all income. An alternative assumption that the remaining income of an educated person in the first period, hy, is not subject to income taxation is considered in Appendix 4.3. If the rate of interest is denoted r, then the present value of net lifetime earnings of the ith person, if investing in higher education, V_i^E, is given by:

$$V_i^E = hy_i(1-t) - c(1-\rho) + y_i(1+s_i+g)(1-t)/(1+r). \qquad (4.1)$$

It is not necessary to assume that the private cost of higher education is all paid in the first period. It could be financed by a loan, to be repaid with interest in the second period; the present value is the same whichever assumption is made, so long as capital markets are perfect. The effects of imperfect capital markets on wealth inequality in a single period framework have been examined by Hare and Ulph (1982). Notice that the net fee, $c(1-\rho)$, is not tax-deductible; in the present framework, with proportional taxation, the effect of allowing higher education expenses to be tax-deductible is equivalent to an increase in ρ.

It is assumed that the cost of education per person, c, is the same for all individuals and remains constant as the number of individuals who are educated increases. It might, however, be argued that in view of the existence of many fixed costs, the average cost per student would be expected to fall. The implications of decreasing costs are examined in Appendix 4.2, where it is seen that the major results are unchanged. Hence this additional interdependence is ignored in what follows.

The present value of net lifetime earnings of those who do not invest in higher education, V_i^N, is given by:

$$V_i^N = y_i(1-t) + y_i(1+g)(1-t)/(1+r). \qquad (4.2)$$

The ith individual is assumed to choose higher education if $V_i^E > V_i^N$. As explained in Chapter 1, there is some value of y_i, called the *educational choice margin*, for which $V_i^E = V_i^N$. All those with y below this margin will not choose to invest in higher education. Equating (4.1) and (4.2) and rearranging gives:

$$\frac{s_i(1-t)}{1+r} + \{(h-1)(1-t)\} - \frac{c(1-\rho)}{y_i} = 0. \qquad (4.3)$$

Suppose, as in Chapter 3, that s_i is proportional to the individual's endowment, y_i, so that:

$$s_i = uy_i \qquad (4.4)$$

This assumption is consistent with observed age-earnings profiles in the sense that they are steeper for those with higher lifetime incomes. It is assumed that the value of u remains constant as ρ is allowed to vary. However, it might be argued that the private returns to higher education would be expected to fall as the proportion of people investing in higher education increases. For this reason the sensitivity of the results to variations in the value of u will be examined in detail. Substituting (4.4) into (4.3) gives the educational choice margin, y^*, as the root of the quadratic:

$$y^{*2}u\left\{\frac{1-t}{1+r}\right\} + y^*\{(h-1)(1-t)\} - c(1-\rho) = 0. \qquad (4.5)$$

Further analysis shows that (with t and $\rho < 1$) there will always be one negative and one positive root of this quadratic, but only the positive root is relevant. When $t = 1$, the educational choice margin is indeterminate. Notice that the general growth rate, g, does not affect the value of y^* since all individuals, irrespective of their education, are assumed to benefit equally from growth. In terms of a diagram such as Figures 1.1 or 3.1, an increase in the external effect of higher education will shift both the V^E and V^N schedules upwards such that the point of intersection still implies the same value of y^*. However, the tax base is higher, so that the proportional tax rate is correspondingly lower.

   The value of y^* can be obtained from (4.5), given values of u, h, ρ, r, c and t. However, t is endogenous as it depends on the proportion of people who receive education, which in turn depends on y^*. It is therefore useful to consider the relationship between y^* and t, for given values of the other parameters. In Chapter 1, this relationship was called the *educational choice schedule*. Examples of this schedule are shown in Figure 4.1. The important question naturally arises of how the model is to be 'calibrated'. Given the two-period nature of the model, a rather high rate of interest is appropriate, though comparisons are not actually influenced by its value. The direct cost of higher education must be specified in relation to other values, particularly the median ability or income level and the level of non-education government expenditure. In all calculations it will be assumed that the median value of y is arbitrarily set at 10, and other values are set in relation to this. Available data and estimates can provide only a very rough guide to

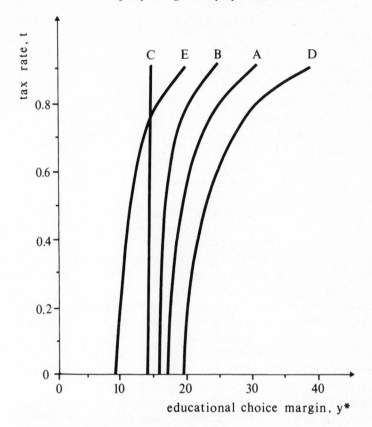

Figure 4.1   Educational choice schedules

appropriate orders or magnitude, and some experimentation is initially required in order to produce sensible values for such endogenous variables as the proportion investing in higher education and the associated tax rate. It should also be borne in mind that the emphasis is always on the comparative static properties of the model, rather than any particular set of absolute values. In schedule A the parameter values are: $c=3$, $u=0.1$, $h=0.1$, $\rho=0$, $r=0.6$. Increasing the value of ρ directly reduces the costs to individuals of investing in higher education and the schedule shifts to the left; schedule B shows the effect of raising ρ to 0.5.

It can be seen that the schedule is slightly steeper as ρ increases and when $\rho=1$ the tax rate has no effect on educational choice; this is shown as schedule C. The explanation for this is that when there are no fees at all, the proportional tax affects all income equally. This result can also be seen by substituting for $\rho=1$ in equation (4.5), giving:

$$y^* = (1 - h)(1 + r)/u \tag{4.6}$$

which is independent of t. At values of ρ less than unity the tax has a greater effect at the higher ranges of t because the cost of education, c, has to be met out of post-tax income. Increasing the cost of education makes it less attractive and therefore raises the educational choice margin, as shown in schedule D. If the private returns to education rise, caused by a rise in u, the choice margin falls. This shifts the educational choice schedule to the left, as in schedule E, and causes the slope to increase slightly. The change in the slope is much less than that caused by the increase in ρ because now all income and costs are affected equally. So at higher tax rates the effect of a higher u will be more marked than at lower tax rates.

The above approach to the investment decision is based on the maximization of net lifetime income where individuals are assumed to know the effect of higher education on subsequent earnings; that is, they know the value of u in determining $s_i = u y_i$. This can be interpreted in terms of individuals being risk neutral, with the value of u as the conditional mean, for given y_i, of a distribution. It might be argued that in practice uncertainty about future returns plays a significant role in educational choice. The difficulties of dealing with uncertainty in the present framework are therefore discussed briefly in Appendix 4.4.

Rates of Return

The total cost of investing in higher education for the ith person during the first period is equal to the sum of forgone earnings net of tax and the direct cost, and is therefore equal to:

$$y_i(1 - t)(1 - h) + c(1 - \rho). \tag{4.7}$$

The net benefit from the investment is the difference between the second period's post-tax income if investing and that obtained when not investing. It is therefore given by:

$$y_i(1 + s_i + g)(1 - t) - y_i(1 + g)(1 - t) = y_i s_i(1 - t). \tag{4.8}$$

The rate of return for the ith person, r_i, is that rate which equates the cost with the present value of the net benefit. Hence dividing (4.8) by $1 + r_i$, equating this to (4.7) and rearranging gives:

$$r_i = \frac{u y_i}{(1 - h) + c(1 - \rho)/\{y_i(1 - t)\}} - 1. \tag{4.9}$$

This result shows how the rate of return increases with the ability level, y_i. At the educational choice margin, where $y_i = y^*$, the rate of return is of course equal to the market rate of interest, r. It is also important to recognize that it is not appropriate simply to substitute alternative parameter values into (4.9) in order to examine the variation in rates of return. Variations in u, h or c will lead to variations in t and ρ via the general equilibrium effects and the endogeneity of government policy.

Many empirical studies have attempted to estimate the 'rate of return' to investment in higher education – the literature is much too extensive to list here. These studies typically produce a single rate which is based on average earnings profiles, with seldom any discussion of the distribution of rates of return. It is difficult to interpret the results, which do not correspond to an average rate of return. Furthermore, government policies often have different impacts on the rates of return close to the educational choice margin and those for very high ability levels (an example will be provided in Chapter 8). Those close to the margin are the most relevant from the point of view of policy analysis.

4.2   THE GOVERNMENT'S BUDGET CONSTRAINT

It is next necessary to obtain the tax rate required to finance the higher education grant. This depends on the proportion, p, of individuals who invest in higher education and thus receive the grant, which in turn is equal to the proportion of people with $y_i > y^*$. Let $F(y)$ denote the distribution function of y, so that $F(y)$ measures the proportion of individuals with endowment less than or equal to y. Hence the proportion who invest in higher education is given by:

$$p = 1 - F(y^*). \tag{4.10}$$

The total cost of financing higher education, per member of the cohort, is equal to pc, or $\{1 - F(y^*)\}c$, of which a proportion, ρ, is given in grant form and is financed by general taxation. But additional government expenditure must also be financed from income taxation. Suppose that the revenue per person required to finance non-education expenditure is equal to the fixed amount R. Hence taxation must raise an amount per person equal to R_t, given by:

$$R_t = \rho c\{1 - F(y^*)\} + R. \tag{4.11}$$

In view of the proportionality of the tax system, in order to obtain R_t it is only necessary to derive the tax base in each period. If N is the number of individuals in the cohort, the total income in the first period is equal to N multiplied by:

$$\int_0^{y^*} y\mathrm{dF}(y) + \int_{y^*}^{\infty} hy\mathrm{dF}(y). \tag{4.12}$$

The first term in (4.12) is the income of those below the educational choice margin while the second term is the income of those with higher education. In the second period, the total income of those not receiving higher education is the same as that obtained by this group in the first period, with the addition of the general growth in incomes resulting from the external effect arising from higher education. It is therefore simply the first term in (4.12) multiplied by $(1+g)$. The total income of those who do invest in higher education is given by N multiplied by:

$$\int_{y^*}^{\infty} (1+uy+g)y\mathrm{dF}(y) \tag{4.13}$$

$$= (1+g)\int_{y^*}^{\infty} y\mathrm{dF}(y) + u\int_{y^*}^{\infty} y^2\mathrm{dF}(y). \tag{4.14}$$

More convenient expressions for total income in the two periods can be obtained using the concept of the incomplete moment distribution of y. The jth moment distribution of $F(y)$ is written as $F_j(y)$ and defined by:

$$F_j(y) = \frac{\displaystyle\int_0^y v^j\mathrm{dF}(v)}{\displaystyle\int_0^{\infty} v^j\mathrm{dF}(v)}. \tag{4.15}$$

Total income of this group in the first period then becomes N multiplied by:

$$\bar{y}\{h+(1-h)F_1(y^*)\}. \tag{4.16}$$

The derivation of the total income of those with $y > y^*$ in the second period is a little more tedious and involves the second moment distribution, so it is given in Appendix 4.1. It is equal to N multiplied by:

$$\bar{y}[(1+g)+u\bar{y}(\eta_y^2+1)\{1-F_2(y^*)\}] \tag{4.17}$$

where $\bar{y}$ is the arithmetic mean of y and η_y is the coefficient of variation. The deficit neutrality condition can now be established. Total expenditure of N

multiplied by R_t must be equal to the present value of tax payments, since a single cohort is being considered in isolation. Rewrite (4.17) as $\bar{y}\psi$, where ψ is the term in square brackets in (4.17). The deficit neutrality condition then gives the required tax rate as:

$$t = \frac{R + \rho c\{1 - F(y^*)\}}{\bar{y}\{h + (1-h)F_1(y^*) + \psi/(1+r)\}}. \tag{4.18}$$

Total tax revenue may be rewritten as:

$$R_t = \xi t \bar{y} \tag{4.19}$$

where $\xi = h + (1-h)F_1(y^*) + \psi/(1+r)$. In a more usual context of a proportional tax system and a single period, the obvious expression for total revenue per person is that $R_t = t\bar{y}$. Equation (4.19) differs from this because of the two-period nature of the model and the fact that the cohort has to be divided into two groups in determining the second period's tax base. Equation (4.18) therefore allows t to be determined, given the values of R, ρ, c, r, y^* and the form of the distribution of y, along with the relationship between the external effect, g, and the proportion investing, p. The latter relationship must now be specified explicitly.

The Growth Rate

A convenient form of $g(p)$ which depends on only one parameter is:

$$g = \delta\left(\frac{p}{1+p}\right). \tag{4.20}$$

Thus g increases from zero, when $p=0$, to $\delta/2$ when everyone invests in higher education. Since $dg/dp = \delta/(1+p)^2$ the rate of increase in g decreases as p increases. Unfortunately, there are few empirical studies which link the proportion with higher education directly to the growth rate, but there has been much work on estimating the social return to education. The large literature on 'growth accounting' may be used indirectly to shed some light on the growth component of the present model.

Distributional Assumptions

The relationship between t and y^*, for given values of the other parameters of the model, has been called the *deficit neutrality schedule* in Chapter 1. But before it is possible to solve equation (4.18), the form of the distribution function F(y) must be specified. The above expressions could be evaluated using any form of F(y) that has convenient first and second moment distributions. Suppose that y is lognormally distributed as $\Lambda(y|\mu, \sigma^2)$ where μ and σ^2 are respectively the mean and variance of the logarithms of y. As shown in Aitchison and Brown (1957), the jth moment distribution of the lognormal, Λ_j, is given by:

$$\Lambda_j(y|\mu, \sigma^2) = \Lambda(y|\mu + j\sigma^2, \sigma^2). \tag{4.21}$$

The lognormal has the property that $\bar{y} = \exp(\mu + \frac{1}{2}\sigma^2)$, with $\eta_y^2 = \exp(\sigma^2) - 1$ and a median of $\exp(\mu)$. The required lognormal integrals can be evaluated using the polynomial approximation given by Aitchison and Brown (1957).

In considering numerical values, the cost of higher education and the amount of non-education government expenditure per capita have to be set in relation to average income; the absolute values chosen are rather arbitrary. It was decided to obtain results for a distribution of y having a median value of 10. The coefficient of variation was set at 0.5, which is a reasonable approximation for industrialized countries. This implies that the lognormal distribution has a variance of logarithms of 0.223 with an arithmetic mean of 11.1795.

Deficit Neutrality Schedules

It is now possible to obtain alternative deficit neutrality schedules using numerical methods. Some examples are shown in Figure 4.2. Of particular interest are the effects of changes in the private returns to higher education, determined by u, and the external effect as influenced by the parameter δ. Schedules A, B and C are drawn for the same values of u, h, c and r as in schedule A of Figure 4.1, with the additional assumptions that $\delta = 1.25$ and $R = 4$. As discussed briefly in the previous section, the various parameter values are chosen in order that they have the appropriate relationship to the assumed median value of y, and give sensible values of p and t when the full model is solved. The emphasis is on comparative statics, rather than absolute values. The schedules are drawn for ρ values of 0, 0.5 and 1 respectively. An increase in ρ has two conflicting effects on this schedule. First, the 'costs effect' is simply the increase in government revenue required. This increase arises from the need to fund a greater proportion of the costs of students already investing in higher education, combined with the effect of the higher number investing as a result of the lower educational choice margin. Secondly, there is a 'tax base effect' caused by the increase in incomes of the extra individuals who become educated, plus the general

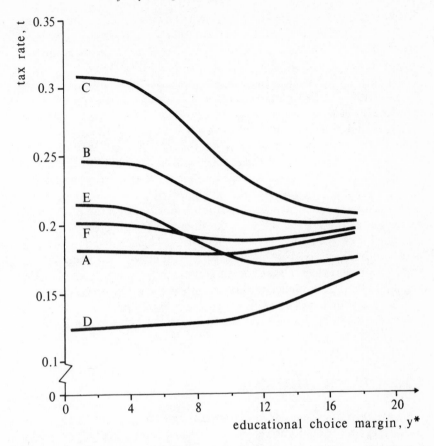

Figure 4.2   Deficit neutrality schedules

increase in incomes arising from the higher external effect. This raises the tax base and provides more revenue at a given rate of tax. The direction of movement in the revenue neutrality schedule as ρ increases therefore depends on the relative size of these effects. The 'cost' effect typically outweighs the 'tax base' effect, thus rendering higher education investment a cost from the government's perspective, as discussed in Chapter 1. This is true except where the choice margin is very high, and very few people receive the grant.

It is useful to refer to the additional expenditure (and hence tax revenue) required to fund a higher proportion of the cost of higher education as representing a negative rate of return to the government's 'investment' in education. This can be contrasted with each individual's rate of return, which must be positive. The next section will compare the median voter's return (that is the return to the median voter from funding a grant for higher education) with the generally negative returns to the government's investment.

Schedules D and E show the effect on the deficit neutrality schedule of increasing the private return to education. As expected, raising the return raises the tax base and shifts the function downwards. When u is higher, the schedule exhibits a different shape for higher values of ρ. At high values of the choice margin the schedule starts to turn upwards, as in schedule F. The tax rate required for revenue neutrality with a given level of funding is higher if the choice margin is higher. The higher choice margin implies that there are fewer individuals investing in higher education; here the government's return to investment in education is positive because of the high contribution to the externality of the high-ability educated individuals combined with their high personal returns to higher education. In this situation the tax base effect outweighs the cost effect. This phenomenon occurs for lower values of the choice margin as the private returns increase. Increasing the cost of higher education shifts the schedule upwards, with a greater effect for lower educational choice margins. This is because the lower margin implies a greater proportion educated and therefore a greater 'cost effect'.

4.3 SOLVING THE MODEL

For a given set of values of u, h, ρ, c and r, the educational choice schedule, giving the educational choice margin for alternative tax rates, can be determined using equation (4.5). For a specified distribution of y and values of δ and R, the deficit neutrality schedule can be determined from equation (4.18).

As shown above, the deficit neutrality schedule is very flat while the educational choice schedule is very steep. Despite the non-linearity of the schedules there is a single point of intersection giving the solution to the model. This gives the combination of the choice margin and the tax rate where, given individual choices, the required tax revenue is raised. It may be said that this implies consistency between all individuals investment decisions and the investment decision of the state. In other words, the tax rate which individuals take as given, and which determines the educational choice margin, is equivalent to the tax rate which raises precisely the amount of revenue needed to pay the state's proportion of each person's education cost in the form of an unconditional grant.

In view of the non-linearity of the model and the need to use a numerical, rather than a graphical, procedure to solve for t and y^*, a two-step iterative method was adopted. This is described as follows. First, an arbitrary tax rate, t_1, is chosen and equation (4.5) is used to calculate the corresponding educational choice margin y^*. This latter value is then substituted into equation (4.18) in order to determine the corresponding tax rate, t_2. If t_1 does not equal t_2, the value of t_1 is re-set to $t_1 + (t_2 - t_1)/2$. This process continues until $t_2 = t_1$, that is, until the procedure converges to a unique tax rate and choice margin.

The above procedure is used for a given value of ρ. The educational status of the median voter can then easily be determined. It can be confirmed that the median person does not invest by comparing the resulting value of the choice margin, y^*, with the median value of y, given by $\exp(\mu)$. In realistic cases the median voter will not invest in higher education. The net lifetime income of the median voter can then be obtained using equation (4.1). By comparing the values of net lifetime income for alternative values of ρ it is possible to find the value of ρ that maximizes the net lifetime income of the median voter, for given values of the other parameters.

Although it is convenient to concentrate on the position of the median voter for the determination of the majority choice of ρ, it is important to recognize that all of those who do not invest in higher education share a common interest. This is because they share equally in the general growth of earnings that results from the higher education of a minority of individuals and because the tax system is proportional. Hence there is a consensus among all of the non-educated concerning their preference for a particular value of ρ.

4.4 SOME NUMERICAL EXAMPLES

It has been seen in earlier chapters that comparative static results can in most cases not be established without considering a more fully specified model. This section therefore uses the numerical procedure described in the previous section to produce a variety of numerical examples. Some results are shown in Table 4.1, for values of r and δ of 0.6 and 1.0 respectively. The table presents the value of ρ chosen by the median voter along with the resulting proportion educated and the proportional tax rate, under a variety of conditions. For example the median voter's preferred value of ρ is 0.8 when $u = 0.08$, $c = 3$, $h = 0.1$ and $R = 4$. The table also shows the corresponding values of p and t in the absence of a grant. The parameter values have been chosen to indicate the implications for relatively high and low values of each variable.

Table 4.2 shows the effect of increasing δ to 1.25. Comparison of the two

Table 4.1 *Majority voting and the higher education grant*

δ = 1.00

		u = 0.08				u = 0.12			
		c = 3		c = 6		c = 3		c = 6	
h = 0.1									
R = 4	ρ	0.80	0	0.40	0	0.15	0	0.05	0
	p	0.090	0.052	0.046	0.030	0.202	0.187	0.120	0.115
	t	0.2161	0.208	0.215	0.211	0.185	0.182	0.190	0.188
R = 8	ρ	1.0	0	0.70	0	0.60	0	0.50	0
	p	0.106	0.042	0.058	0.021	0.245	0.160	0.157	0.089
	t	0.424	0.419	0.428	0.426	0.377	0.368	0.390	0.384
h = 0.3									
R = 4	ρ	0.75	0	0.40	0	—[a]	0	0.025	0
	p	0.185	0.103	0.089	0.056	—	0.287	0.177	0.174
	t	0.213	0.199	0.211	0.205	—	0.169	0.178	0.177
R = 8	ρ	0.95	0	0.70	0	—	0	0.4	0
	p	0.221	0.083	0.117	0.039	—	0.250	0.213	0.136
	t	0.413	0.402	0.420	0.415	—	0.342	0.370	0.363

Note: [a] These values imply p > 0.5 and are therefore not reported.

Table 4.2 Majority voting with a higher externality

$\delta = 1.25$

			u=0.08				u=0.12			
			c=3		c=6		c=3		c=6	
h=0.1										
R=4		ρ	1.0	0	0.65	0	0.55	0	0.30	0
		p	0.107	0.052	0.063	0.030	0.256	0.187	0.151	0.116
		t	0.218	0.207	0.219	0.211	0.194	0.180	0.195	0.187
R=8		ρ	1.0	0	0.90	0	0.85	0	0.65	0
		p	0.107	0.042	0.085	0.021	0.303	0.162	0.193	0.090
		t	0.420	0.417	0.431	0.424	0.379	0.364	0.392	0.381
h=0.3										
R=4		ρ	1.0	0	0.65	0	—[a]	0	0.25	0
		p	0.238	0.104	0.127	0.056	—	0.288	0.218	0.174
		t	0.221	0.198	0.219	0.204	—	0.166	0.185	0.175
R=8		ρ	1.0	0	0.80	0	—	0	0.55	0
		p	0.238	0.083	0.144	0.039	—	0.251	0.260	0.135
		t	0.409	0.400	0.421	0.413	—	0.337	0.372	0.359

Note: [a] These values imply $p > 0.5$ and are therefore not reported.

71

tables shows the high degree of sensitivity of the majority choice of ρ to the value of δ. The results indicate the extent to which the majority choice of ρ increases with δ, and there is a wide range of situations where the grant is the whole of the fee.

From each table it can be seen that as the direct cost of education, the fee c, increases, the majority choices of ρ decreases. This is not surprising, but it is of interest to consider the comparative statics further. First, for any given value of ρ, the educational choice schedule shifts to the right as c increases, while the deficit neutrality schedule shifts upwards as the higher cost increases the tax rate for a given choice margin. In view of the flatness of the deficit neutrality schedule, the new point of equilibrium implies a higher tax rate and higher choice margin for a given value of ρ.

In ascertaining the median voter's likely response, in terms of the preference for ρ, it is as before necessary to consider the effect of changing ρ on the marginal cost and benefit in terms of net lifetime income. Before the increase in c the marginal cost and marginal benefit were equal. To the median voter the marginal cost of increasing ρ is the extra tax incurred, while the marginal benefit arises from the growth of second-period income. The growth rate is an increasing but marginally diminishing function of the proportion educated. Therefore a rise in c which, *ceteris paribus*, leads to fewer people investing in higher education, means that the marginal effect on the external rate of raising ρ is greater. Therefore the marginal benefit from providing a tax-financed grant rises. However, the marginal cost will rise by much more than the benefit. First, as argued above, the tax rate is higher as a result of the increase in c; secondly, the tax base declines as the educational choice margin rises; hence obtaining a given change in ρ will be more expensive. The effect on the marginal cost far outweighs the increase in the marginal benefit for a given change in p. Hence the majority choice of ρ decreases as the cost of education increases.

Increasing the private returns to education, by increasing u, lowers ρ and the grant unless the median voter is educated. From each table it can be seen that when u is raised from 0.08 to 0.12 the majority choice of funding falls as long as p is less than 0.5. The effect of increasing u can be more clearly understood by considering its effects on the educational choice and deficit neutrality schedules. Increasing u makes higher education attractive from an individual's perspective and therefore shifts the educational choice schedule to the left. With higher private returns the tax base will be larger, so for given ρ and p the tax rate will be lower. This shifts the deficit neutrality schedule downwards. The net outcome of these two shifts is that for a given ρ the choice margin is unambiguously lower whereas the tax rate may vary either way. However, a reduction in the tax rate is the most likely outcome. Although the fiscal rate of return is negative this will generally be more than compensated by the tax revenue generated by the effect on the tax base of both growth and the higher private returns. This holds except where both ρ and p are high; here the public good aspect is small and therefore a rise in the number educated raises the tax rate.

Consider next the choice of grant by the median voter, at a higher value of private benefits reflected by u. The fiscal rate of return is generally negative, so as the grant is increased the tax rate must rise (except on the rare occasion where the proportion educated is very low). Before the rise in u the median voter preferred that level of grant at which the marginal benefit is equal to the marginal cost. The marginal benefit to the median voter of increasing ρ comprises the increase in the external benefit, g, along with an increase in the tax base which places downward pressure on the tax rate. The marginal cost of raising the grant arises from the increase in the amount of revenue the state must raise and the consequent increase in the tax rate. To ascertain the median voter's response to the change, it is necessary to investigate its effect on these marginal values.

When u increases, more individuals choose to become educated, so for a given level of ρ, p is higher. With the marginal effect of p on the external benefit diminishing as p increases, the marginal benefit to the median voter from an increase in the grant is now lower. So the marginal benefit from funding has fallen. At the higher level of u, increasing the grant raises the tax rate by less than before because the tax base is greater. In view of the positive skewness of the distribution of ability, the number responding to the extra funding will not be as great. Therefore the marginal cost to the median voter has fallen. As both the marginal cost and the marginal benefit have fallen it is impossible to predict, *a priori*, the direction of the median voter's response to an increase in u. However, a strong result is that under all conditions examined the median voter supported a reduction in the grant in response to the u increase.

Increasing h has the same qualitative effects as an increase in u; individuals forgo a smaller proportion of their first period earnings so it makes higher education more attractive as an investment and lowers the tax rate required to achieve deficit neutrality at a given choice margin. Its effect on the median voter's preferred level of the grant cannot therefore be predicted *a priori*. However, in all situations increasing h lowers the preferred ρ for the median voter.

An interesting result is that increasing R, the government net revenue requirement, that is expenditure per person not devoted to higher education, always has the effect of increasing the median voter's preferred value of the grant and of increasing the proportion investing. This may initially seem paradoxical considering that the fiscal rate of return is negative; the median voter favours the government increasing expenditure on higher education when other expenditure is increasing, thereby putting further extra upward pressure on tax rates. To explain this, consider again the effects on the two schedules. The choice margin is unaltered directly by any changes in R. However, the deficit neutrality schedule shifts upwards. The new intersection implies that for a given ρ there is a higher tax rate and a higher choice margin. In order to understand the median voter's preference it is again necessary to compare the marginal effect of changes in ρ both before and after the increase in R. With R higher, both the tax rate and the educational choice margin are higher for a given ρ, so the proportion investing is smaller. The effect of diminishing marginal returns is now opposite to that which occurs when u increases; the effect is that the marginal benefit from an increase in ρ is higher.

On the cost side, increasing ρ raises the tax rate but with a higher R, the tax rate rises by proportionately less. This is because those who invest in higher education in response to the higher grant contribute more to the tax base than before the increase in R. Combined with the fact that the tax rate is higher, the increase in the tax base contributes proportionately more to total revenue. Therefore the marginal cost of increasing the grant falls. With the fall in the marginal cost and the rise in the marginal benefit, it is in the interests of the median voter to vote for a higher value of grant. In considering this result it must, however, be recognized that no allowance has been made for the effects on individuals of the government expenditure resulting from the revenue of R per person. A more complete model would have higher education as just one component of government expenditure and would need to consider the full implications of the other components. But this would by no means be a trivial extension of the present analysis.

APPENDIX 4.1   THE DEFICIT NEUTRALITY SCHEDULE

This appendix provides further details concerning the derivation of the deficit neutrality schedule of equation (4.18). First, total income in the first period, given in equation (4.12), can be simplified to N multiplied by:

$$\bar{y}\{h + (1-h)F_1(y^*)\}. \tag{4.22}$$

This uses the first moment distribution $F_1(y)$ obtained by substituting $j = 1$ in the general form given in (4.15). In examining income in the second period, the first term in (4.14) is also simplified using the first moment distribution and is equal to N multiplied by $(1+g)\{1 - F_1(y^*)\}$. But the second term requires the second incomplete moment distribution, $F_2(y)$, which from the general definition in (4.15) is given by:

$$F_2(y)\frac{\displaystyle\int_0^y v^2 dF(v)}{\displaystyle\int_0^\infty v^2 dF(v)}. \tag{4.23}$$

The denominator of (4.23) is the mean squared deviation about the origin. If $V(y)$ denotes the variance of y, then by using the standard result that:

$$V(y) = \int (y - \bar{y})^2 dF(y) = \int y^2 dF(y) - \bar{y}^2 \tag{4.24}$$

the denominator of (4.23) can be written in terms of the mean and variance of y as $V(y) + \bar{y}^2$, or $\bar{y}^2(\eta_y^2 + 1)$, where η_y denotes the coefficient of variation of y. The expression in (4.14) is thus simplified to:

$$(1 + g)\bar{y}\{1 - F_1(y^*)\} + u\bar{y}^2(\eta_y^2 + 1)\{1 - F_2(y^*)\}. \tag{4.25}$$

The calculations use the lognormal distribution, which has the convenient relation between moment distributions given by (4.21). In calculating the appropriate lognormal integrals, the polynominal approximation given in Aitchison and Brown (1957, p. 71) was used.

APPENDIX 4.2   VARIATIONS IN THE COST OF EDUCATION

This appendix examines the effect of varying the direct cost per student, that is the fee, as the proportion of individuals in the cohort who invest in higher education increases. It is more realistic to assume that as p rises the cost of education falls. A major reason for this is the existence of high fixed costs. The cost variation may be specified by the following function:

$$c = d_1(p + \theta)^{-d_2}. \tag{4.26}$$

This implies that increasing d_2 and reducing θ raises the variation in the cost for given changes in p while d_1 changes only the absolute size of the cost without changing the variability. The major implication for the mechanics of the model is that the educational choice schedule is rather more complex

Table 4.3   *Majority voting with cost reductions*

δ=1, r=0.6			A				B			
			$d_1=2.25, d_2=0.6, \theta=0.1$				$d_1=3, d_2=0.4, \theta=0.1$			
			$u=0.08$		$u=0.12$		$u=0.08$		$u=0.12$	
$h=0.1$	$R=4$	ρ	0.55	0	0.55	0	0.5	0	0.35	0
		p	0.050	0.026	0.223	0.124	0.049	0.026	0.177	0.125
		t	0.2187	0.213	0.204	0.187	0.216	0.212	0.197	0.187
	$R=8$	ρ	0.85	0	0.85	0	0.8	0	0.70	0
		p	0.075	0.014	0.288	0.087	0.069	0.017	0.230	0.092
		t	0.433	0.429	0.396	0.384	0.431	0.427	0.392	0.383
$h=0.3$	$R=4$	ρ	0.85	0	0.5	0	0.7	0	—[a]	0
		p	0.187	0.046	0.36	0.223	0.145	0.053	—	0.211
		t	0.230	0.206	0.192	0.173	0.222	0.205	—	0.174
	$R=8$	ρ	1	0	—	0	0.9	0	—	0
		p	0.238	0.027	—	0.164	0.190	0.034	—	0.160
		t	0.430	0.420	—	0.356	0.427	0.417	—	0.357
			when $p=0.1$, $C=5.9$				when $p=0.1$, $C=5.71$			
			when $p=0.2$, $C=4.63$				when $p=0.2$, $C=4.85$			

Note: [a] These values imply $p > 0.5$ and are therefore not reported here.

76

and the numerical procedure for solving the model has to be modified accordingly. However, convergence is again easily achieved.

In making comparisons with the constant cost case reported above, it is necessary to ensure that, over the relevant range of p, the values of c are similar. Some results are given in Table 4.3, for alternative values of the parameters d_1, d_2, and θ. Values of c corresponding to p of 0.1 and 0.2 are reported at the foot of the table. In each case the values of δ and r are set at 1.0 and 0.6 respectively.

It can be seen that when ρ is low the proportion educated is generally lower than in comparable cases with fixed costs. This is primarily due to the existence of a very high cost at low values of p, which for low ρ are borne entirely by the students. However, as ρ increases, p rises rapidly so that the median voter's preferred value of ρ the proportions educated are similar to those found in the constant cost case.

In general a large increase in the proportion investing which accompanies an increase in ρ has two effects. First, as already noted, the cost falls rapidly; secondly, the external benefit g rises more rapidly. In some cases these effects can combine to produce a positive fiscal rate of return; that is, the tax rate required in order to achieve deficit neutrality falls as ρ rises. However, this is most unusual and the case of a negative fiscal rate of return is normal.

If the incentive to invest in higher education is initially very low and then rises, by an increase in either u or h, it may be in the interests of the majority to support a higher value of ρ. This result, although always conceptually possible, was never observed in the case of fixed average costs. With variable costs it is observed that, for all the reported increases in h, the preferred value of ρ rises; the only exception is when u is high, as here the value of p with $\rho = 0$ is so high that the effects on p of increasing ρ are small. Furthermore, if p is low and the private returns rise, the preferred value of ρ is seen to rise.

The most interesting result concerns the effect on the median voter's choice of ρ of the extent to which c varies with p. By varying the shift parameter, d_1, in order to maintain values of c for the relevant range of p at similar levels, the parameters θ and d_2 can be varied in order to isolate effects of changes in the variability of the cost with p. By comparing the values of the preferred ρ, it can be seen that the median voter is prepared to support a higher level as the variation in the cost per student increases. Results show that increasing the rate of decline in cost, even if the absolute cost is higher for a given p, often leads to the median voter's support for a higher value of ρ.

Table 4.4 *Majority voting with alternative tax treatment*

$\delta = 1.25$

		u=0.08				u=0.12			
		c=3		c=6		c=3		c=6	
h=0.1									
R=4	ρ	0.775	0	0.45	0	0.65	0	0.35	0
	p	0.20	0.120	0.112	0.071	0.265	0.178	0.151	0.109
	t	0.213	0.196	0.212	0.201	0.210	0.191	0.209	0.198
R=8	ρ	0.85	0	0.60	0	0.775	0	0.60	0
	p	0.231	0.111	0.128	0.058	0.303	0.165	0.187	0.089
	t	0.408	0.394	0.413	0.406	0.401	0.385	0.414	0.402
h=0.3									
R=4	ρ	0.325	0	0.225	0	—[a]	0	0.175	0
	p	0.285	0.227	0.165	0.130	—	0.304	0.214	0.181
	t	0.201	0.190	0.204	0.195	—	0.185	0.200	0.191
R=8	ρ	—	0	0.325	0	—	0	0.30	0
	p	—	0.245	0.190	0.124	—	0.317	0.243	0.170
	t	—	0.379	0.401	0.392	—	0.368	0.395	0.384

Note: [a] These values imply $p > 0.5$ and are therefore not reported.

APPENDIX 4.3   ALTERNATIVE TAX TREATMENT OF EDUCATED INDIVIDUALS

A slight modification of the above model would be to assume that the remaining income, hy, of an educated person in the first period is not subject to income tax. To some extent the first period income, if educated, may be regarded as an intra-family (inter-generational) transfer. In this case equation (4.1) becomes:

$$V_i^E = hy_i - c(1-\rho) + y_i(1+s_i+g)(1-t)/(1+r). \qquad (4.27)$$

The educational choice margin, y^*, is then given as the positive root of:

$$y^{*2}u(1-t)/(1+r) + y^*\{h - (1-t)\} - c(1-\rho) = 0 \qquad (4.28)$$

when $\rho = 1$ it is easily seen that:

$$y^* = (1 - t - h)(1 + r)/(1 - t)u. \qquad (4.29)$$

Hence the educational choice schedule is, unlike the case considered above, not vertical in the special case of full state funding of education. Equation (4.29) only holds for $t + h < 1$, and shows that the educational choice schedule is 'backward bending' with y^* decreasing as t increases. This occurs essentially because, when t is high and there are no direct education costs to be met, the untaxed first period income makes education much more attractive than otherwise.

An implication of the backward-bending educational choice schedule is that anything which shifts the deficit neutrality schedule downwards, such as an increase in δ, will lead to an increase in y^* and hence a *decrease* in the proportion of the cohort investing in higher education. For a larger fixed grant an increase in the extent to which education raises the growth rate will actually reduce the demand for higher education. But it must be recognized than an increase in δ may also lead to majority support for a higher value of ρ, which has the effect of reducing y^*. Examples are shown in Table 4.4.

APPENDIX 4.4   UNCERTAIN RETURNS

The analysis has assumed that individuals know with certainty the effect of higher education on earnings during the remainder of the working life. As suggested above, the approach can be interpreted as assuming risk neutrality with each s_i interpreted as a conditional mean for given y_i. Unfortunately, the introduction of uncertainty with risk aversion creates rather intractable problems in the present framework. For example, re-write equation (4.1) as:

$$V_i^E = a_i + b_i s_i \qquad (4.30)$$

with $a_i = h y_i(1-t) - c(1-\rho) + y_i g(1-t)/(1+r)$ and $b_i = y_i(1-t)/(1+r)$. Suppose that the utility function takes the form $U(V^E) = (V^E)^a$, so that the expected utility from investing in higher education for the ith individual is given by:

$$E[U(V_i^E)] = \int (a_i + b_i s_i)^a dF(s|y_i) \qquad (4.31)$$

where $F(s|y_i)$ is the distribution function of s conditional on the value of y. The presence of the term a_i in (4.31) complicates the expression significantly. If $a = 2$, the expected utility will obviously depend on the mean and variance of the conditional distribution of s, otherwise higher-order and fractional moments are involved. In view of this complexity, the assumption of certainty is retained.

5. Progressive income taxation and social welfare

Previous chapters have concentrated on majority voting in the context of a proportional income tax. This chapter examines the government's decision regarding the level of a higher education grant under alternative assumptions about the government's objective and the income tax system. The use of a social welfare function which explicitly involves a trade-off between efficiency and equity is considered and compared with the decision that receives majority support. In each case a proportional tax is compared with an income tax system involving a tax-free threshold and a single marginal tax rate applied to income measured above the threshold. It is seen that majority voting over the level of the grant is more complicated with progressive income taxation compared with a proportional tax, though a voting equilibrium can be obtained in specific examples.

The plan of the chapter is as follows. The individual investment decision is described in section 5.1 along with the government's budget constraint. Section 5.2 then examines voting equilibria with alternative tax systems. The maximization of a social welfare function, whose arguments include the arithmetic mean value of net lifetime income and a measure of inequality, is examined in section 5.3. In section 5.4 attention is shifted to preferences regarding the income tax structure itself, rather than the higher education grant.

5.1   A PROGRESSIVE INCOME TAX

This section derives the educational choice and deficit neutrality schedules when there is a progressive income tax. The model is otherwise the same as that discussed in Chapter 4, so it is described only briefly in order to establish the notation.

The Investment Decision

Individuals invest in higher education so long as the rate of return exceeds the rate of interest; that is, if the after-tax present value of lifetime earnings with higher education, V^E, exceeds the present value of earnings without higher education, V^N. The cost of investing in higher education to an individual includes the value of earnings forgone during the first period when education takes place, plus the direct cost in the form of fees, less any government grant. If capital markets are perfect it does not matter whether the fees are financed by borrowing, and the following analysis assumes that fees paid are not tax-deductable.

If an individual does not invest in higher education in the first period, earnings are equal to y. If educated, a proportion $1 - h$ of such earnings are forgone. As explained earlier, the value of y is determined by an individual's income-earning ability which also influences the ability to benefit from higher education. The value of y varies between individuals and follows the distribution function $F(y)$. The private benefits of higher education are reflected in the assumption that earnings in the second period are increased by a proportion, s, which itself depends on the individual's value of y; the simplifying assumption is made that $s = uy$, where u is a constant that applies to all investing individuals.

The external effect of higher education involves an increase in productivity, and hence a proportional increase in real earnings, by an amount, g, for all individuals in the cohort. The extent of this external effect is assumed to depend on the proportion of the cohort that invests in higher education. Denote the cost of education per person by c, and suppose that there is a government grant of ρc, available to all individuals who invest in education. The private calculations will of course also be influenced by the rate of interest, r, and the nature of the income tax system. The latter is described in terms of a tax-free threshold, a, and a single marginal tax rate, t, applied to income measured above the threshold.

Consider the present value of net lifetime income for educated and uneducated individuals. In the case of a proportional tax it was only necessary to consider the two sets of individuals, those above and below the educational choice margin. However, the existence of the tax-free threshold complicates the analysis. There are two groups of individuals who invest in higher education, and three groups of those who are below the educational choice margin. First, notice that if income is above the threshold, the tax paid is equal to $t(y - a)$ and net income is therefore equal to $at + y(1 - t)$. The system is thus equivalent, for taxpayers, to one in which an unconditional transfer payment, at, is received and there is a proportional tax applied to all income.

For those investing in higher education with $hy \leq a$, who therefore pay no tax in the first period, net lifetime income is given by:

$$V^E = hy - c(1 - \rho) + \{at + y(1 + s + g)(1 - t)\}/(1 + r) \qquad (5.1)$$

while those investing, with $hy > a$, pay tax in both periods and have a net lifetime income of:

$$V^E = at + hy(1-t) - c(1-\rho) + \{at + y(1+s+g)(1-t)\}/(1+r). \quad (5.2)$$

Those who do not invest in higher education fall into three groups. For those with $y \leq a$ and $y(1+g) \leq a$, no tax is paid at any time and net lifetime income is simply:

$$V^N = y + y(1+g)/(1+r). \quad (5.3)$$

For $y \leq a$ and $y(1+g) > a$, tax is paid only in the second period, so that:

$$V^N = y + \{at + y(1+g)(1-t)\}/(1+r). \quad (5.4)$$

Finally, those with $y > a$ pay tax in both periods, giving:

$$V^N = at + y(1-t) + \{at + y(1+g)(1-t)\}/(1+r). \quad (5.5)$$

Since the grant is the same for all those who invest in higher education and the private benefits are assumed to be monotonically related to y, there is some value of y, say y^*, above which investment takes place. This has been referred to in previous chapters as the educational choice margin. In order to solve for the educational choice margin, several sets of calculations may be necessary because it is important to check that the resulting value of y^* is consistent with the assumptions made about incomes in each period in relation to the tax-free threshold. First, equate (5.1) and (5.5) and rearrange, using $s = uy$, to get:

$$y^2 u(1-t)/(1+r) + y\{h - (1-t)\} - \{c(1-\rho) + at\} = 0. \quad (5.6)$$

The positive root of this quadratic gives the value of the margin, y^*, so long as it is less than a/h, since (5.1) applies only for $hy \leq a$. If this condition does not hold, then equate (5.2) and (5.5) to get:

$$y^2 u(1-t)/(1+r) + y(1-t)(h-1) - c(1-\rho) = 0. \quad (5.7)$$

The positive root of (5.7) gives the value of y^* so long as it is greater than a/h. Notice that (5.7) does not depend directly on the tax-free threshold, a, although of course in the complete solution of the model the marginal tax rate, t, depends on the value of the threshold chosen. It is convenient to write:

$$y^* = y^*(a, t, \rho, c, h, u, r) \qquad (5.8)$$

which defines the educational choice schedule. The terms c, h, u and r are exogenously fixed along with the distribution function $F(y)$, while the values of a, t and ρ must be decided by the government. As before, it is assumed that education is not rationed, so that supply is demand-determined; a supply constraint has been discussed in Chapter 1. Each individual's decision is made independently of other individual's plans. However, the government must set the level of the grant and the tax system in order to ensure that its objectives are achieved, subject to the appropriate tax revenue being generated in order to finance the grant. This constraint is examined in the following sub-section.

The Budget Constraint

The problem facing the government is to set the values of a, t and ρ which achieve its objective, subject to the constraint that the expenditure on higher education is fully financed from tax payments. Individual's decisions must generate a tax base that is capable of raising the required revenue. If government revenue needed to finance other forms of expenditure is in present value terms given by R per member of the cohort, then total tax revenue which must be raised per person is equal to:

$$R + \rho c \{1 - F(y^*)\}. \qquad (5.9)$$

The term $1 - F(y^*)$ represents the proportion, p, of the cohort which invests in higher education. The government's budget constraint requires that the present value of tax payments per person is equal to expenditure given by (5.9).

The calculation of total tax revenue is complicated by the fact that five separate groups of individuals discussed above need to be considered. Among those who do not invest, there are some people who pay no tax in both periods, some who pay tax in both periods, while others pay tax in the second period if the external benefit from higher education takes them above the tax-free threshold in the second period. The final two groups comprise those who invest in higher education and pay tax in both periods, and those who do not pay tax in the first period.

In view of the extra complexity, the derivation of the government budget constraint is given in Appendix 5.1, but here it is sufficient to note that the constraint allows the marginal tax rate, t, to be determined for given values of the other variables. Hence, it is possible to write the deficit neutrality schedule as:

$$t = t(a, y^*, c, h, u, r, g, R). \tag{5.10}$$

Furthermore, as in previous chapters, it is assumed that the function relating the external benefit to the proportion investing in higher education, $g = g(p)$, takes the form $g = \delta p/(1 + p)$.

The model has therefore been reduced to the form which is familiar from the previous chapter. Equations (5.8) and (5.10) define the educational choice and deficit neutrality schedules respectively. The intersection of the two schedules gives the simultaneous determination of t and y^*, for given values of a, ρ and so on. This can be achieved numerically using a modification of the iterative process described in Chapter 4. The procedure can of course be repeated for alternative combinations of parameters, and of particular interest are the results for variations in ρ.

5.2 MAJORITY VOTING OUTCOMES

One approach to modelling the government's decision-taking process is to assume that the government chooses the option that would receive majority support, and that individuals support that level of ρ which maximizes their net lifetime income. As explained in Chapter 1, each individual, with given value of y, has a preference profile which relates net lifetime income to the value of ρ. It is required to choose a value of ρ, which determines (with c) the size of the higher education grant, for a given value of the tax-free threshold, a, and the other parameters of the model. In general a choice must be made about the size of the tax-free threshold and other forms of government expenditure, but the following analysis concentrates on the single-dimensional problem of the choice of ρ. Voting over multi-dimensional issues is known to create difficult existence problems. In the final section of the chapter, attention will however be focused on the choice of tax-free threshold for a given value of the grant.

An increase in ρ will induce a reduction in the educational choice margin and require an increase in tax revenue. The higher tax rate required to finance the increase in ρ will impose a cost on all those who do not invest in higher education, as well as on those who do invest; the latter cost can be regarded as a deferred payment of part of the grant. The cost will differ for each individual, but will depend on the extent to which higher education raises the tax base, which is influenced by both the private and the public returns to higher education. Those who do not invest will be prepared to vote for the increase in ρ so long as the increase in their incomes, generated by the external effect of higher education as measured by g, compensates for the extra tax they must pay. At some stage the effect of the concavity of $g(p)$

combined with the rising cost of education as y^* falls will mean that no further increase in ρ is desired. Some minimum value of the parameter δ will be required to generate support for a grant; the mere existence of an externality is necessary but not sufficient.

As ρ rises and y^* falls, some individuals who would not previously have invested in higher education cross the educational choice margin, so that their interests are then aligned with those of the educated and they will benefit from further increases in ρ. Thus it can be seen that those who cross the choice margin at some stage (and who would not invest in higher education when ρ is zero or quite low) have double-peaked preference profiles. They prefer either a relatively low value of ρ when their tax burden is small and they are uneducated, or a high value when they themselves benefit from higher education but pay higher taxes. The implications of double-peaked preference profiles for a majority voting equilibrium under proportional and progressive taxation are different, and are treated separately below.

A Proportional Income Tax

Under a system of proportional taxes, for which the tax-free threshold is zero, it has already been established in earlier chapters that those who do not invest in higher education are unanimous in their preferred level of higher education funding. In maximizing net lifetime income, given by $y\{1+(1+g)/(1+r)\}(1-t)$ for those below the educational choice margin, g and t will themselves depend on the value of ρ, but differentiation of net lifetime income with respect to ρ will give a first-order condition that is independent of y. Thus the level of ρ that is preferred by a representative uneducated individual will be preferred by all of the uneducated, irrespective of their value of y. Hence, with proportional taxes, double-peaked preference profiles do not pose difficulties for majority voting, since the majority of the population does not invest in higher education and they all prefer the same value of ρ. Under a proportional tax, a stable voting equilibrium exists. It is convenient to concentrate on the preferences of the individual with the median value of y, who in realistic cases will not invest in higher education. This individual can without ambiguity be referred to as the median voter.

A Progressive Income Tax

With a progressive tax system, there is no longer unanimity among those below y^*. Those with lower incomes, especially those below the threshold in both periods, will prefer to see ρ increase beyond the value preferred by the individual with the median value of y. For an individual below the educational choice margin and with $y > a$, the value of net lifetime income is equal to $y\{1 + (1 + g)/(1 + r)\}(1 - t) + at\{1 + 1/(1 + r)\}$ where, as before, g and t depend on ρ. The existence of the second term in the expression for net lifetime income means that the first-order condition for maximization with respect to ρ will depend on the value of y, so those who are below the choice margin will not be unanimous in their preferred level of ρ.

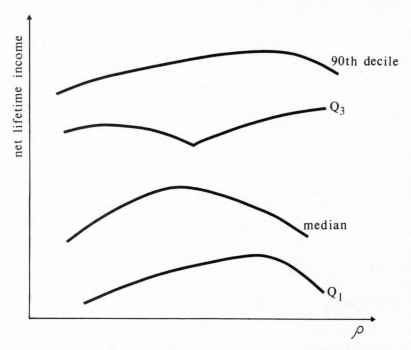

Figure 5.1 Variations in lifetime income with progressive taxation

Figure 5.1 illustrates the variation in net lifetime income with ρ, for various deciles of the population, where the tax-free threshold is positive. This shows that the preferred level of ρ of individuals in the lower deciles is higher than that of the individual with the median value of y. Unlike the proportional tax case, it does not seem possible to establish a general result concerning the existence of a majority voting equilibrium. However, by examining in detail the preference profiles of various percentiles of the distribution of y, it is usually possible to find a value of ρ which is supported by a stable majority of the cohort. This majority value cannot be associated with the preferences of a particular percentile and will depend on the particular parameters of the model. It will involve a coalition being formed between the high and low income groups. For example, it is possible to find a coalition of high- and low-income individuals preferring a value of say $\rho = 0.70$ which constitutes a majority, whereas the individual with median y may prefer a lower value of, say 0.65. This coalition comprises highly endowed individuals who favour a higher value of ρ because they benefit directly from the grant, along with individuals with low y who also favour a higher value of ρ because they bear little or none of the tax cost while still sharing in the external benefit.

A voting equilibrium can be determined for alternative values of the tax-free threshold. In general, it is found that the majority choice of the grant increases with the tax-free threshold. As the tax-free threshold increases and the tax is shifted towards the higher income groups, a larger grant is required in order to induce any given proportion of the cohort to invest in higher education. Similarly, more individuals in the lower tail of the distribution of income will pay no tax at all. The result is that as the threshold increases, the associated majority choice of the grant increases.

5.3   TRADE-OFF BETWEEN EQUITY AND EFFICIENCY

It has been seen that as the progressivity of the tax system increases, so that the costs of a higher education grant can be shifted to higher income groups, the majority choice of the grant increases. The increase in the grant enables more individuals, though still a minority of the cohort, to obtain private returns from higher education and simultaneously increases the external benefit that accrues to everyone. But the majority choice will stop short of the value of the grant that maximizes the arithmetic mean value of net lifetime income; the latter will reach a maximum when the total costs equal the total benefits of the grant.

The grant is made to those who invest in higher education, and are therefore more highly paid, so it is regressive, even if those below the margin benefit to some extent from the existence of a tax-financed grant. An increase in the grant is thus typically associated with an increase in the relative dispersion of net lifetime income. However, when there is a tax-free threshold (associated with lower dispersion), increases in the grant beyond very high values will ultimately lead to a reduction in the dispersion of net lifetime income as the proportion of the cohort above the educational choice margin becomes very large. Such large values are therefore of no practical relevance.

A Social Welfare Function

The above argument suggests that a government which aims to maximize the mean value of net lifetime income (and hence its total value) will give a larger grant than under the voting equilibrium. But the higher total income is obtained at the cost of a greater degree of inequality. Hence it is of interest to consider the behaviour of a government which maximizes a social welfare function involving a trade-off between a measure of inequality and the arithmetic mean, or between 'equity and efficiency'. It is therefore very useful if a social welfare function can be written in 'abbreviated form' in terms of just two variables, an inequality measure and arithmetic mean income. Instead of arbitrarily writing welfare as a simple function of a chosen inequality measure and mean income, it seems preferable to begin with a welfare rationale from which the abbreviated function, and its associated inequality measure, can be derived explicitly. Several different welfare functions have been shown to lead to abbreviated social welfare functions containing the well-known Gini measure of inequality; for a discussion of the general issues involved, see Lambert (1993). However, the following analysis uses the Atkinson (1970) inequality measure and its associated welfare function.

The well-known Atkinson measure of inequality is very useful because it can be related directly to a welfare function in which social welfare, W, is defined as the sum of individual utilities, $\sum_i U(z_i)$. Here the utility function, U, is imposed by the decision-taker rather than being regarded as each individual's function, and z_i is person i's post-tax net lifetime income. Alternative forms of U may of course be examined, but Atkinson used the familiar form:

$$U(z_i) = \frac{z_i^{1-\epsilon}}{1-\epsilon} \qquad \text{with } \epsilon \neq 1 \qquad (5.11)$$

$$= \log z_i \qquad \text{with } \epsilon = 1. \qquad (5.12)$$

The parameter, ϵ, measures the constant degree of relative 'inequality aversion' of the decision-taker. The derivative, $\partial U/\partial z$ is equal to $z^{-\epsilon}$ and the weight attached to higher incomes in the social welfare function decreases as ϵ increases. For $\epsilon = 0$ the government simply maximizes total (or average) net lifetime income.

If z_e is that level of income which, if equally distributed, would generate the same social welfare as the actual distribution, then Atkinson's inequality measure, $I(\epsilon)$ is defined as:

$$I(\epsilon) = 1 - z_e/\bar{z}. \tag{5.13}$$

Hence with N individuals:

$$NU(z_e) = \sum_i U(z_i) = W$$

and

$$z_e = \left(\frac{1}{N} \sum_i z_i^{1-\epsilon} \right)^{1/(1-\epsilon)}. \tag{5.14}$$

The nature of the trade-off implied by the use of $I(\epsilon)$ is therefore immediately obtained from the definition in (5.13) and the result in (5.14). The combination of these two equations shows that welfare per person, W/N, can be expressed as:

$$\frac{W}{N} = \frac{[\bar{z}\{1 - I(\epsilon)\}]^{1-\epsilon}}{1-\epsilon}. \tag{5.15}$$

This gives the abbreviated social welfare function, such that welfare per person is a convenient function of mean post-tax income, $\bar{z}$, and the measure of inequality. The government is regarded as attempting to maximize (5.15) subject to the relationship between $\bar{z}$ and $I(\epsilon)$ implied above, for a specified value of ϵ. Clearly, the higher is the value of ϵ, the further the optimum is from the maximum value of $\bar{z}$. It can be seen that the slope of indifference curves implied by (5.15) is given by:

$$\frac{d\bar{z}}{dI(\epsilon)} = \bar{z}\{1 - I(\epsilon)\}^{-1}. \tag{5.16}$$

The trade-off is precisely the same as the abbreviated welfare function given simply by $\bar{z}\{1 - I(\epsilon)\}$, which is just the equally distributed equivalent income. This more convenient form is therefore often used instead of (5.15).

The maximization of the social welfare function, subject to the relevant constraint, can be viewed in terms of a tangency solution involving social indifference curves in the $\bar{z}$, $I(\epsilon)$ space. The government aims to reach the highest social indifference curve possible. The nature of the constraint, involving the relationship between $\bar{z}$ and $I(\epsilon)$ implied by the model presented above, is very complex and can only be examined in detail using numerical methods. However, it is clear that, over the feasible range, a rise in the grant leads to a rise in inequality, the extent of which depends upon the measure of inequality aversion. It will also be expected to lead to a rise in mean post-tax income up to a point, beyond which further increases in ρ are unequivocally undesirable as they lead to a rise in inequality whilst reducing arithmetic mean post tax lifetime income. Further discussion of inequality is provided in Chapter 7.

Proportional Taxation

Consider first the maximization of social welfare under proportional taxation. The relationship between $\bar{z}$ and $I(\epsilon)$, that is the constraint facing the government, implied by the model is numerically calculated and shown in Figure 5.2, schedule CC, for $\epsilon = 1.2$. The parameter values used in the calculations are as follows: $\delta = 1.0$; $r = 0.6$; $h = 0.2$; $u = 0.1$; $R = 6.0$ and $c = 4.0$. This distribution of y is, as before, assumed to be lognormal with a median of 10.0 and a coefficient of variation of 0.5. It can be seen that schedule CC reaches a maximum at the point B which represents that level of inequality corresponding to the highest arithmetic mean post-tax lifetime income. Social welfare will be maximized, for a given ϵ, at a point where the social indifference curve, shown as schedule W, is a tangent to the trade-off relationship; this is the point A in Figure 5.2. This is obviously less than that level of funding which would maximize mean post-tax income.

The schedules in Figure 5.2 were obtained numerically for illustrative purposes, but for the purposes of calculating the value of ρ which maximizes social welfare a numerical search procedure is used involving the direct calculation of the welfare function in the form $W = \sum_i U(z_i)$ with U given by (5.12). It is obviously much easier numerically to search for the value of ρ which maximizes W than to obtain numerical approximations to tangents in an attempt to find the tangency solution. Furthermore, this involves using a simulated population of individuals (from the specified distribution of ability, y). The reported results are based on a random selection of 15,000 individuals. Figure 5.2 also illustrates the way in which measured inequality is related to the value of ρ.

With a higher degree of inequality aversion of $\epsilon = 2.0$ the trade-off will shift to the right, as in schedule $C'C'$. This is because, for a given level of the grant and hence a given income distribution, a higher inequality aversion parameter leads to a higher measure of inequality. With a higher ϵ the tangency will occur at a lower level of funding, because the social welfare function is more willing to trade income increases for reduced inequality. Table 5.1 shows variations in the majority choice of ρ for alternate values of ϵ. Notice that a value of ϵ of 5.2 leads to a socially preferred value of ρ, equal to 0.55, which is approximately the same as under the voting equilibrium. Thus the process of majority voting determines a level of ρ

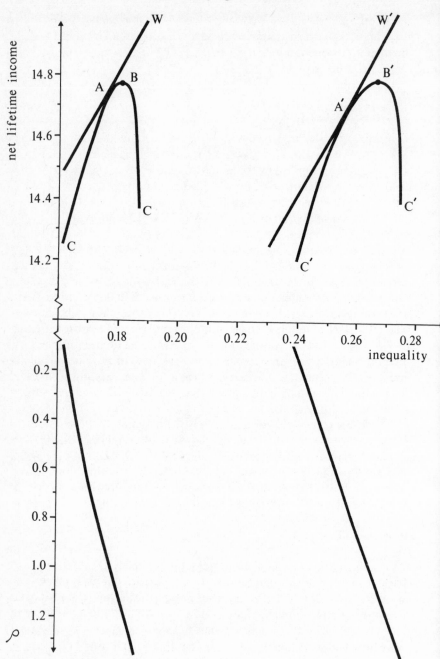

Figure 5.2   Maximum social welfare

Table 5.1   *The grant and inequality aversion: proportional taxation*

Basis of government decision	ρ
Majority voting	0.54
Social welfare function with:	
$\epsilon = 0$	1.0
$\epsilon = 0.5$	0.96
$\epsilon = 1.2$	0.87
$\epsilon = 2.0$	0.73
$\epsilon = 4.0$	0.59
$\epsilon = 5.2$	0.55

which would also maximize social welfare if there is a very high degree of inequality aversion.

An aversion to inequality of about 5 is extremely high and implies that in the social welfare function considerable emphasis is given to those with relatively low incomes. It might initially be though that the maximization of a social welfare function, even for much lower degrees of relative inequality aversion, would imply a lower grant than that chosen by majority rule. This might be suggested because the median voter has no concern for inequality, and a higher grant is associated with higher lifetime inequality. However, the median voter also has no concern for aggregate net lifetime earnings, given that with a positively skewed distribution the arithmetic mean exceeds the median value. Furthermore, the difference between the arithmetic mean and the median increases as the grant increases, because of the increase in relative dispersion which affects the mean but not the median. When these considerations are kept in mind, there is thus nothing very surprising about the fact that majority voting typically results in a lower grant than the maximization of a social welfare function.

Progressive Taxation

The process of determining a welfare maximum, that is a tangency between social indifference curves described by (5.15) and the trade-off, can be repeated under a system of progressive taxes. However, under progressive taxes the trade-off is altered. In general, an increase in ρ will lead to a smaller rise in inequality as tax progression ensures that increases in ρ are financed more heavily by the more highly endowed. Indeed, it is found that for high values of ρ, that is, above approximately 1.2, the value of $I(\epsilon)$ begins to decrease as ρ is increased further. This implies that the trade-offs corresponding to those in Figure 5.2 begin to bend backwards and downwards. However, this range is not important as only the positively sloped part is relevant.

Table 5.2   *The grant and inequality aversion: progressive taxation*

Tax-free threshold	Max. mean net lifetime income	Social welfare function with: $\epsilon = 1.2$	$\epsilon = 2.0$
1	1.00	0.95	0.84
2	1.00	0.97	0.93
3	1.05	1.04	0.99
4	1.20	1.20	1.17

Table 5.2 lists values of ρ which maximize mean post-tax income and social welfare, for $\epsilon = 1.2$ and 2.0 under progressive income taxation. For a given threshold, columns 2 and 3 demonstrate the decline in the optimal levels of ρ with a rise in inequality aversion. This generally follows the results obtained for the case of proportional taxation; however, as the tax threshold rises the divergence between the value of ρ which maximizes mean income and that which maximizes social welfare, for a given ϵ, declines. With a tax threshold of 4, the value of ρ which maximizes social welfare, for $\epsilon = 1.2$, equals that level which maximizes mean post-tax income. This result could be interpreted as suggesting that, with a greater degree of progressivity in the tax system, the tax system alone achieves the distributional aims, and the higher education grant attempts to satisfy the independent objective of maximizing arithmetic mean, and therefore total, income. But it is clear from the above results that in general these policy objectives cannot be pursued independently.

Comparison with Earlier Studies

Some of the results may be compared with earlier studies of financing higher education. For example, Green and Sheshinski (1975) also analysed government funding of higher education, where a positive externality is generated, under the assumption that the goverment maximizes a utilitarian social welfare function. However, they took the amount available for higher education funding as exogenous and found that increases in this given amount lead to a more regressive distribution of government funds. Furthermore an increase in the size of the externality generated by higher education also leads to a more regressive distribution. A significant difference from the present study is that there is no consideration given to the financing of the higher education subsidy. The model developed here analyses the revenue requirement of the government and thus is also able to model the choice of the amount of funding in the light of the government's budget constraint. Nevertheless, it has been found that the inclusion of a revenue requirement reinforces Green and Sheshinski's (1975) results as a comparison of marginal costs and benefits of increasing the tax-financed grant shows that regressive higher education funding increases with an increase in the externality generated by higher education.

The analysis of the marginal costs (through the tax system) of increasing the higher education grant may be compared with the approach taken by Ulph (1977). He finds that, in order to maximize total income for a given level of inequality aversion, progressivity in the tax and transfer system is complemented by regressivity in the distribution of education subsidies. Ulph models the disincentive of high marginal tax rates and finds that if society's distributional objectives are achieved through the tax system then the consequent loss in income can be redressed by increasing the subsidy to higher education. Although Ulph's (1977) consideration of aspects of the progressivity of the tax system is an attempt to draw connections between state funding of higher education and the system of taxes, he does not model the government's budget constraint. Furthermore Ulph does not consider the effects of taxes and higher education subsidies on individuals' invest-ment decisions, nor the implications of an externality generated by educa-tion. However, the present approach, which allows for these extra interde-pendencies, reinforces Ulph's results. A rise in the progressivity of the tax system leads to a decline in the incentive to invest in higher education, so higher education enrolments fall. However the dependence of the external benefit generated by higher education on the proportion educated implies that it becomes more profitable for the government to finance higher education through the tax system, irrespective of its objective. Thus, as found by Ulph, higher education funding becomes more regressive.

5.4 TAX PREFERENCES

The emphasis has so far been on the government's choice of a grant, given the nature of the tax system and allowing for changes in the marginal tax rate required to satisfy the budget constraint. But it is possible to use the present framework in order to examine the nature of individuals' prefer-ences regarding the tax structure, in particular the value of the tax-free threshold, for given values of the higher education grant. It is well established that preferences over progressive taxes are likely to be double-peaked, giving rise to potential problems from the point of view of public-choice mechanisms. However, Roberts (1977) has shown, in a single-period context, that a voting equilibrium exists if changes in the tax system do not change the rankings of individuals when ordered by post-tax income. The present context is one in which the rankings are indeed preserved, but it involves two periods rather than one. Furthermore, individuals have the opportunity, through investment in higher education, to shift taxable income between the two periods to some extent.

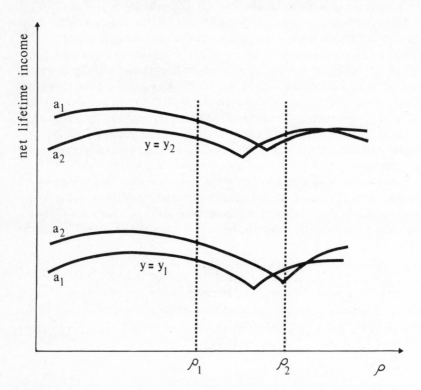

Figure 5.3   Choice of income tax schedule

Suppose that the tax structure has a tax-free threshold, a, and a constant marginal rate, t. Figure 5.3 illustrates net lifetime income for two individuals, i and j where $y_i < y_j$, under tax-free thresholds a_2 and a_1, where $a_1 < a_2$. These individuals' net incomes always have the same ranking. The horizontal axis specifies values of ρ which are for present purposes assumed to be exogenously set. The values used in the numerical derivation of Figure 5.3 are specified in Appendix 5.2.

Each profile has a similar pattern. Net lifetime income increases as ρ increases, even though at values of y, of y_1 and y_2, individuals do not themselves invest in higher education. The external benefit resulting from the greater proportion educated, as ρ increases, combines with the increase in the tax base to ensure that the necessary increase in the marginal tax rate does not outweigh the benefit of the higher number investing. But as ρ increases further the additional tax outweighs the growth effect and the profiles turn downwards until ρ is sufficiently high to make it worthwhile, at that level of y, to invest in higher education. The profile then abruptly turns upwards. When ρ is equal to ρ_1, neither individual is educated and the person with $y=y_1$ prefers the higher tax-free threshold and higher associated marginal tax rate, while the person with $y=y_2$ prefers the lower threshold. When, however, $\rho=\rho_2$, both individuals invest in higher education but y_1 is such that $hy_1<a_1$, while $hy_2>a_1$. It can be seen from Figure 5.3 that, given ρ_2, the person with y_2 prefers a *higher* value of a and the person with the lower value of y of y_1 prefers a *lower* tax-free threshold. The explanation for this apparent paradox hinges on the fact (not obvious from Figure 5.3) that $hy_1<a_1$ but $hy_2>a_1$. This result can be explained by further considering the determinants of net lifetime income.

Suppose that with a particular value of ρ, and the other parameters of the model, investment in higher education by a particular individual is not worthwhile. Such an individual's net lifetime income, where $y>a$, is given by:

$$V=y(1-t)+at+\frac{y(1+g)(1-t)+at}{1+r} \tag{5.17}$$

where r is the rate of interest at which the second period's earnings are discounted. Differentiation of V with respect to the threshold, a, and rearranging, gives:

$$(1+r)\frac{\partial V}{\partial a}=(2+r)t+\frac{\partial t}{\partial a}\left[(2+r)a-y\left\{2+r+g-(1-t)\frac{\partial g}{\partial t}\right\}\right]. \tag{5.18}$$

The term $\partial g/\partial t$ reflects the extent to which the external benefit, obtained by all individuals, changes as the tax rate increases. Since an increase in the marginal tax rate will reduce the proportion of people who find it worthwhile to invest in higher education, then $\partial g/\partial t$ must be negative. Whether or not $\partial V/\partial a$ is positive depends unambiguously on the value of y. As y increases there must be some value at which $\partial V/\partial a$ turns from positive to negative. Thus among individuals who are below the educational choice margin, those with relatively low incomes will vote for an increase in the tax-free threshold while those with higher incomes will vote for a decrease.

Now suppose that, with a higher value of ρ, an individual invests in higher education, but the value of y is such that $hy < a$ and no tax is paid in the first period. Then net lifetime income is:

$$V = hy - (1-\rho)c + \frac{y(1+s+g)(1-t)+at}{1+r}. \qquad (5.19)$$

Differentiation of (5.19) with respect to the threshold, a, and rearrangement gives:

$$(1+r)\frac{\partial V}{\partial a} = t + \frac{\partial t}{\partial a}\left[a - y\left\{1+s+g-(1-t)\frac{\partial g}{\partial t}\right\}\right]. \qquad (5.20)$$

Again $\partial g/\partial t < 0$ and it is clear that there can be some value of y, say y^+, above which $\partial V/\partial a < 0$ and such individuals prefer a reduction in the tax-free threshold, a. Furthermore, since an individual's educational investment depends upon the tax system, with higher marginal tax rates acting as a disincentive, increases in a, and therefore t, reduce the proportion educated. Individuals who are thus dissuaded from investing will not obtain the grant. Thus if the rise in the threshold leads to them not being educated, net lifetime income is calculated using (5.17) instead of (5.19). Thus at a given ρ there will be some initially educated individuals who will not favour an increase in the tax threshold as this, in effect, removes their transfer payment in the form of the grant, ρc.

However, it is important to recognize that equation (5.20) only applies to values of y such that $hy < a$. For higher values of y, tax must be paid in the first period and net lifetime income is given by:

$$V = hy(1-t) + at - (1-\rho)c + \frac{y(1+s+g)(1-t)+at}{1+r}. \qquad (5.21)$$

In this case:

$$(1+r)\frac{\partial V}{\partial a} = (2+r)t + \frac{\partial t}{\partial a}\left[(2+r)a - y\left\{1+s+g+(1+r)h-(1-t)\frac{\partial g}{\partial t}\right\}\right]. \qquad (5.22)$$

Again it is clear that the sign of $\partial V/\partial a$ in (5.22) depends on the value of y. There is some value, say y^{++}, above which $\partial V/\partial a < 0$ and such individuals would vote for a decrease in the threshold. Also from (5.22) it is clear that for a given individual $\partial V/\partial a$ depends on the absolute value of t. Thus a rise in the threshold is more likely to be preferred if t is initially high. With a higher t, raising the tax-free threshold yields a larger effective 'tax credit', equal to at. Thus even for relatively high income individuals there will be some level of ρ, with implied t, that is high enough to ensure that income rises with the tax threshold. Therefore over the range of ρ there are some relatively high income individuals, $y > y^+$, for whom $\partial V/\partial a$ in (5.22) is positive. At the same time there will be individuals, with $y < y^+$ and $hy < a$, who benefit from a *decrease* in the threshold; that is, for whom $\partial V/\partial a$ in (5.20) is negative. However, because of the existence of the factor $(2 + r)$ in the first term in (5.22) and within the square brackets, it is quite possible to have $y^{++} > y^+$.

These lower-income individuals do not benefit from a rise in progression as the consequent rise in marginal tax rates acts as a disincentive to their investing in higher education, thus reducing their transfer payment (the grant). For a given ρ, some higher-income individuals will however prefer a higher a. There is an incentive for some of those with relatively high incomes to form a coalition with the relatively low-income groups to vote for an increase in the tax-free threshold beyond the level preferred by the median voter. A stable majority can indeed be found, but it does not include the median voter. The ranking of individuals is always preserved; the identity of the median voter is unchanged whatever the value of ρ. But the majority voting outcome cannot be identified with the preferences of the median voter. This differs from the important result established by Roberts (1977) for voting over progressive taxes in a single period context. This issue will thus be examined in further detail in the following chapter.

APPENDIX 5.1 TOTAL TAX REVENUE

The tax function used implies that those with income above the threshold pay an amount of tax equal to $t(y - a)$ or $ty - at$. From this it follows that, for any particular group in the income distribution, the total tax revenue obtained from that group is equal to

$$t \left\{ \begin{array}{c} \text{total income of those in} \\ \text{the group with } y > a \end{array} \right\} - at \left\{ \begin{array}{c} \text{number of people in} \\ \text{the group with } y > a \end{array} \right\}.$$

If there are N people altogether, and the arithmetic mean is denoted $\bar{y}$, then the above expression can be written as N multiplied by:

$$ t\bar{y}\left[\left\{\begin{matrix}\text{proportion of total income of}\\ \text{those in the group with } y>a\end{matrix}\right\} - \frac{a}{\bar{y}}\left\{\begin{matrix}\text{proportion of people in}\\ \text{the group with } y>a\end{matrix}\right\}\right]. $$

This general result can be applied to any group within the population, specified by earnings limits. If $F(y)$ denotes the proportion of individuals with income not greater than y, it is convenient to write $F_1(y)$ as the proportion of income of those with incomes not exceeding y; that is, $F_1(y) = \int_0^y w dF(w)/\bar{y}$. This is the incomplete first moment distribution defined in Chapter 4.

Those Not Investing in Higher Education

In the first period, tax revenue is raised from the non-educated with y between the threshold, a, and the educational choice margin, y^*. Hence application of the above general rule shows that the tax raised from this group is $Nt\bar{y}$ multiplied by:

$$ \{F_1(y^*) - F_1(a)\} - \frac{a}{\bar{y}}\{F(y^*) - F(a)\}. \tag{5.23} $$

In the second period, the group of non-educated tax payers includes those who in the first period had $a/(1+g) < y < y^*$. This is because the general growth of earnings, at the rate g, brings those between $a/(1+g)$ and a in the first period into the tax 'net'. Hence the tax raised from the non-educated in the second period is equal to $Nt\bar{y}$ multiplied by:

$$ (1+g)\left\{F_1(y^*) - F_1\left(\frac{a}{1+g}\right)\right\} - \frac{a}{\bar{y}}\left\{F(y^*) - F\left(\frac{a}{1+g}\right)\right\}. \tag{5.24} $$

Those Investing in Higher Education

In the first period, if $hy^* > a$ then all those who invest in higher education will pay tax. Hence the application of the general result shows that total revenue from this group is $Nt\bar{y}$ multiplied by:

$$ h\{1 - F_1(y^*)\} - \frac{a}{\bar{y}}\{1 - F(y^*)\}. \tag{5.25} $$

However, if $hy^* < a$, only those with income above a/h must pay tax. Hence revenue becomes $Nt\bar{y}$ multiplied by:

$$h\left\{1 - F_1\left(\frac{a}{h}\right)\right\} - \frac{a}{\bar{y}}\left\{1 - F\left(\frac{a}{h}\right)\right\}. \tag{5.26}$$

All the educated will pay tax in the second period. Hence it is first necessary to calculate the total second period income of those above y^*. Now, the second period income of an educated person is given by $y(1+s+g) = y(1+g) + uy^2$, since $s = uy$. Hence it is necessary to obtain a convenient expression for $u\int_{y^*} y^2 dF(y)$. This is most easily achieved using the term $F_2(y)$ which is defined as $\int^y w^2 dF(w)/\int w^2 dF(w)$. This is the second incomplete moment distribution defined in Chapter 4. Further, denote the coefficient of variation of y as η_y. The total tax paid by the educated in the second period can then be shown to be equal to $Nt\bar{y}$ multiplied by:

$$(1+g)\{1 - F(y^*)\} + u\bar{y}(1 + \eta_y^2)\{1 - F_2(y^*)\} - \frac{a}{\bar{y}}\{1 - F(y^*)\}. \tag{5.27}$$

The Determination of t

The present value of total tax payments can then be obtained by dividing the sum of (5.24) and (5.25) by $(1+r)$ and adding the result to (5.23) and either (5.25) or (5.26), whichever is applicable. This total must then be multiplied by $Nt\bar{y}$. The budget constraint then requires that revenue be equal to N multiplied by $R + \rho c\{1 - F(y^*)\}$. It is seen that the tax rate enters the resulting equation in an extremely simple way, so that it may be calculated given values of the other variables. For a given value of t (and other variables), the value of y^* can be calculated using the result of section 5.1. The value of t which corresponds to y^* can then be calculated using the results of the present appendix. The process can be repeated until the two values of t are equal. In all the calculations reported here it is assumed as before that y follows a lognormal distribution with a median of 10.0 and a coefficient of variation of 0.5.

APPENDIX 5.2   TAX PREFERENCES

This appendix provides further details regarding the preferences of individuals for alternative progressive tax systems, discussed in section 5.4. The calculations assume that y is lognormally distributed with a median value of 10 and a coefficient of variation of 0.5. Consider the sixth and seventh deciles, d_6 and d_7, equal to 11.27 and 12.81 respectively (the arithmetic mean is 11.1795). If $h = 0.2$, then when individuals with y equal to these deciles are educated, their first period earnings, hy, are 2.25 and 2.56 respectively. Then if $a_1 = 2.4$, the person at the sixth decile pays no tax in the first period. Suppose further that $u = 0.1$, $r = 0.6$, and $\delta = 1.0$. Comparisons of net lifetime income are shown in Table 5.3. It can be seen from the first two rows that when $\rho = 0.6$, and neither individual is educated, the person at the sixth decile prefers an increase in the tax-free threshold from 2.4 to 2.6, while the seventh decile's net lifetime income is lower for the higher threshold. Using information about the proportion educated, it can be seen that $\partial g/\partial t$ is very low for $\rho = 0.6$. However, for $\rho = 1.2$ the more paradoxical situation arises where the preferences of individuals regarding a change in the threshold are reversed. Furthermore $\partial g/\partial t$ is significantly higher with the higher value of ρ; the increase in the threshold from 2.4 to 2.6 produces a smaller increase in the marginal tax rate but a larger fall in the proportion educated. As also shown in section 5.4, the seemingly paradoxical result can only occur when comparing individuals who are both educated and where the lower income individual does not pay tax in the first period.

Table 5.3   Individual choice of tax structure

Tax-free threshold	ρ	Net lifetime 6th decile	Income 7th decile	Proportion educated	Marginal tax rate
2.4	0.6	13.656	15.324	0.179	0.370
2.6	0.6	13.666	15.315	0.178	0.377
2.4	1.2	13.353	15.603	0.420	0.435
2.6	1.2	13.311	15.613	0.408	0.439

Note: $h = 0.2$; $u = 0.1$; $\delta = 1.0$; $c = 4.0$; $R = 6.0$.

6. Majority voting over progressive taxation

In the previous chapter a simple progressive income tax, involving a tax-free threshold and a single marginal rate, was introduced and the implications for majority voting over the level of the higher education grant were examined. The different issue of the public choice of tax system (in terms of the choice of the level of the tax-free threshold), for a given grant, was also considered. It was found that situations can exist in which a relatively high-income individual prefers an increase in the threshold while an individual with a lower income prefers a decrease in the threshold. This apparently paradoxical result was explained in terms of the ability of individuals to shift taxable income between periods by investing in higher education. The important result relating to just a single period, derived by Roberts (1977), establishes that a majority voting equilibrium will exist so long as the rankings of individuals are unchanged for different tax schedules; this condition is referred to as 'hierarchical adherence'. The present chapter therefore digresses slightly from the major theme of the book to consider majority voting over progressive income taxation in more detail. It is useful to establish whether the result obtained in the previous chapter is a special case, or whether a more general qualification to Roberts's result, when extending the framework to more than one period, can be found.

The chapter is organized as follows. Section 6.1 considers the simple case of majority voting over both a negative income tax and a tax schedule with a tax-free threshold combined with a single marginal rate above the threshold, where there are no incentive effects. These simpler cases provide an introduction to the more complex cases involving endogenous incomes. Section 6.2 then sets out the basis of Roberts's (1977) analysis of the structure of preference over taxes when labour supply effects exist. Section 6.3 shows how the approach can be extended to deal with a two-period framework, and provides a simple example of a situation in which hierarchical adherence is not sufficient to produce consistent social choices. The choice of example is suggested by the higher education model used in this book.

6.1   A FIXED PRE-TAX INCOME DISTRIBUTION

This section examines the choice of tax schedule in a single period in two simple cases of a linear income tax and a schedule with a single marginal rate applied to income above a threshold. It considers the extreme situation in which the distribution of income is given independently of the tax schedule. This straightforward case therefore serves as an introduction to subsequent sections.

A Linear Income Tax

Consider a linear income tax in which all income is taxed at the proportional rate, t, and each individual receives an unconditional transfer payment of a, so that the tax paid on an income of y, $(T(y))$, is given by:

$$T(y) = ty - a. \qquad (6.1)$$

The relationship between a and t for which the individual pays a constant amount of tax, T, is thus:

$$a = ty - T. \qquad (6.2)$$

This form of iso-tax schedule for an individual defines a set of indifference curves in a, t space. If y is independent of the tax structure, the individual's choice problem simply involves minimizing the tax paid, subject to the government's budget constraint which requires that the tax system must raise net revenue of say q per capita. Aggregation of (6.1) thus gives the budget constraint as:

$$q = t\bar{y} - a \qquad (6.3)$$

where $\bar{y}$ is arithmetic mean income. Variations in a and t satisfying (6.3) are thus

$$a = t\bar{y} - q. \qquad (6.4)$$

Comparison of (6.2) and (6.4) shows immediately that an individual with $y < \bar{y}$ chooses a corner solution with t set at its maximum value of unity. Hence with a positively skewed distribution of income, the median is less than the mean and majority voting would result in everyone receiving the same after-tax income of $\bar{y} - q$. The individual with $y = \bar{y}$ is of course indifferent between combinations of a and t along (6.4), whereas those with

$y > \bar{y}$ would prefer the corner solution with $a = 0$ and $t = q/\bar{y}$. This simple choice problem is shown in Figure 6.1. Where incentive effects exist the budget constraint (6.4) is no longer linear but concave; however, minimization of the tax paid is no longer an appropriate objective; this case is examined later.

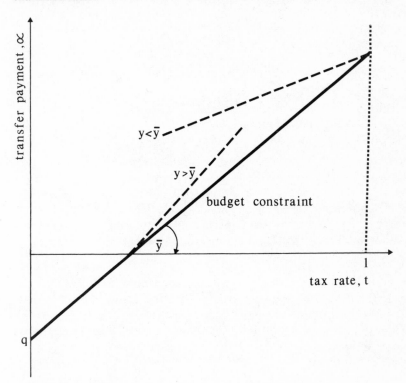

Figure 6.1 A linear income tax

A Tax-free Threshold

Instead of the unconditional transfer payment involved in the linear tax scheme, suppose that there is a tax-free threshold, a, so that, as in Chapter 5, the tax paid is:

$$T(y) = 0 \qquad \text{for } y \leq a$$
$$= t(y - a) \qquad y > a. \qquad (6.5)$$

Total differentiation of (6.5) shows that, for a fixed amount of tax paid by an individual with $y > a$, the relationship between a and t has a slope of:

$$\left.\frac{da}{dt}\right|_T = \frac{y-a}{t}. \tag{6.6}$$

The government's budget constraint is given by:

$$q = t \int_a (y-a) dF(y) \tag{6.7}$$

where $F(y)$ is the distribution function of y. Hence (6.7) reduces to:

$$q = t\bar{y}G(a) \tag{6.8}$$

where

$$G(a) = \{1 - F_1(a)\} - (a/\bar{y})\{1 - F(a)\} \tag{6.9}$$

and $F_1(a)$ denotes the proportion of total income held by those with incomes not exceeding a. The function $G(y)$ has been examined in detail in Creedy (1985), where it is seen to play an important role in the analysis of tax and transfer schemes. Unlike the previous case, the budget constraint in (6.8) is concave with a slope given, after totally differentiating with respect to a and t and setting $dq=0$, by:

$$\left.\frac{da}{dt}\right|_q = \frac{-G(a)}{t\partial G(a)/\partial a}. \tag{6.10}$$

From (6.9) it can be found by differentiating that:

$$\frac{\partial G(a)}{\partial a} = \frac{-\{1 - F(a)\}}{\bar{y}}. \tag{6.11}$$

So that substituting into (6.10) gives the result that along the budget constraint:

$$\left.\frac{da}{dt}\right|_q = \frac{\bar{y}\{1 - F_1(a)\} - a\{1 - F(a)\}}{t\{1 - F(a)\}}. \tag{6.12}$$

From (6.6) and (6.12) there is a tangency position between an individual's iso-tax schedule and the government's budget constraint. In view of the concavity of the individual's iso-tax schedule, this tangency position corresponds to a point of maximum rather than minimum tax liability.

Every individual's iso-tax schedule, for $y > a$, is more concave than the budget constraint. Thus corner solutions are again appropriate for minimizing the tax liability. From (6.5) it is seen that:

$$\frac{dT(y)}{dt} = (y - a) - t\frac{da}{dt}. \tag{6.13}$$

The substitution for da/dt, from the government's budget constraint, from (6.12), into (6.13) shows the change in an individual's tax burden as the individual moves along the government's budget constraint. This gives:

$$\frac{dT(y)}{dt} = y - \bar{y}\frac{\{1 - F_1(a)\}}{\{1 - F(a)\}}. \tag{6.14}$$

Since $F_1(a) < F(a)$ for a positively skewed distribution, (6.14) indicates that all those with $y \le \bar{y}$ would reduce their tax burden by moving upwards along the government's budget constraint to the point where $t = 1$ and the tax-free threshold takes the maximum value given by the root of $q - \bar{y}G(a) = 0$. Thus majority choice would again result in a unit tax rate. Instead of complete equality of after-tax income, all those with incomes above the tax-free threshold have their incomes reduced to the level of the threshold. The median voter therefore pushes the threshold as high as possible consistent with the government's revenue constraint being met. When $a = 0$ and $y > \bar{y}$ it is clear from (6.14) that the individual's tax burden would increase, so that all those above the arithmetic mean would vote for a proportional tax system. The tax-minimizing choice given the tax function of this subsection is illustrated in Figure 6.2. The existence of incentive effects would increase the concavity of the budget constraint.

6.2 ENDOGENOUS INCOMES IN A SINGLE PERIOD

Majority voting over the tax schedules considered in section 6.1 is relatively straightforward where there are no incentive effects of taxes. The essential feature of both cases is that those with relatively high incomes prefer lower tax rates than those with relatively low incomes. A stable majority of individuals can be formed since the alignment of voters is so straightforward. In both of the above cases there is a proportion $F(\bar{y}) > 0.50$ in favour of a unit tax rate because of the positive skewness of the income distribution.

When the distribution of y is no longer exogenously fixed, it is not sensible to take tax minimization as the individual's objective. A more

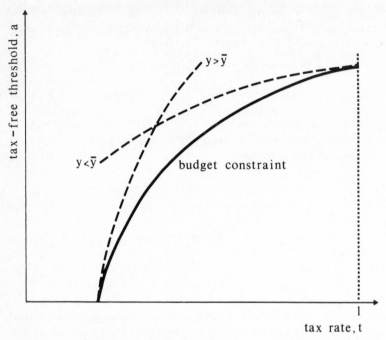

Figure 6.2   A tax-free threshold

appropriate objective is the maximization of utility, considered as a function of post-tax income (equal to consumption if savings are ignored in a static framework) and leisure. The government's budget constraint will be much more concave than in the previous section, since in particular total revenue would be expected to be zero for both zero and unit tax rates. With standard indifference curves a tangency solution, rather than a corner solution, may be regarded as the typical outcome.

The question of whether a stable majority of voters can be formed in favour of a particular combination of tax parameters (satisfying the government's constraint) therefore turns on the question of the way in which individuals are aligned under different regimes. If this alignment or ranking of individuals is not affected by the tax schedule and in addition if higher-income individuals unambiguously prefer lower taxes, then it is intuitively clear that majority voting will produce a stable majority in which the median voter's preferences dominate. The conditions ensure that the identity of the median voter is independent of the tax schedule and that there is no incentive for any individuals who have (endogenous) incomes below the median to form coalitions with any individuals above the median. Hence the median holds the balance of power whatever the tax structure;

the median voter theorem can be applied irrespective of the fact that individuals may have double peaked preferences in terms of their choice of tax rate.

This argument has been stated more formally and much more completely in the context of the linear income tax by Roberts (1977), who describes the stability of the ranking of individuals by income as 'hierarchical adherence'. Roberts also considers a wider choice of voting mechanisms than the simple majority choice system. He examines the existence of a most preferred outcome for mechanisms satisfying decisiveness, neutrality and non-negative responsiveness. Robert argues: 'It is a remarkable feature of the problem under consideration that [hierarchical adherence] is a sufficient condition on preferences for the existence of a choice set to be proved' (1977, p. 334). The remainder of this section briefly describes Roberts's basic argument, leading to his Lemma 1 (1977, pp. 334–5) which concerns preference orderings.

Endogenous Incomes

Assume that individuals vote over the parameters of a linear income tax schedule, where as before t is the marginal tax rate and a is the lump-sum subsidy. The tax paid by individual i with income y_i is given by $T(y_i) = ty_i - a$ and the relationship between t and a such that total government receipts finance fixed net revenue, q, where $\bar{y}$ is mean pre-tax income and n is the number of individuals, is given by $a = t\bar{y} - q/n$.

It is necessary that at any majority voting equilibrium leisure is a normal good, $dt/da|q > 0$, as otherwise everyone can be made better off by a reduction in t. Roberts defines hierarchical adherence as follows: For all i, j: either $y_i(a, t) \leq y_j(a, t)$ for all a, t or $y_i(a, t) \geq y_j(a, t)$ for all a, t, where $y_i(a, t)$ is the pre-tax income that i chooses to obtain under a, t. This implies that there exists a 'natural' ordering of individuals such that pre-tax income is always increasing irrespective of the parameters of the tax and transfer system. In Roberts's model, individuals choose labour supply and therefore income earned, y, in order to maximize utility, which is increasing in net income and decreasing in labour supply, subject to the tax schedule. Hierarchical adherence is effectively a constraint on the form of individuals' utility functions which ensures that labour supply responses are such that the ordering of individuals is preserved across all values of a and t consistent with the government's revenue requirement being met. When preferences are identical this simply requires that the elasticity of hours supplied is not less than 1; in general it would not appear to be unduly restrictive.

Roberts's Lemma 1 states that if $i > j$, that is, $y_i(a, t) > y_j(a, t)$, then for $t_2 > t_1$:

(i) $t_2 I_i t_1$ implies $t_2 P_j t_1$
(ii) $t_2 P_i t_1$ implies $t_2 P_j t_1$

with a being varied to satisfy the budget constraint in each case; see Roberts (1977, p. 344). Hence if an individual prefers a lower to a higher tax rate, all those with a higher income also prefer a lower rate; if an individual prefers a higher to a lower rate, all those below the individual in the hierarchy also prefer a higher rate; if an individual is indifferent between two tax rates, all those above do not prefer a higher rate while all those below do not prefer a lower rate.

The approach to endogenizing incomes involves writing the individual's utility function in terms of consumption and leisure. Assuming that consumption is equivalent to post-tax income and that the wage rate is fixed, that pre-tax income can be regarded as reflecting labour supply. The utility function is written, for the linear tax function, as:

$$U = U(a + y(1 - t), y). \tag{6.15}$$

For given a and t, the individual chooses y (and hence labour supply) in order to maximize U. The first order condition for interior solutions is:

$$(1 - t)U_c + U_y = 0 \tag{6.16}$$

where U_c and U_y refer to partial derivatives of U. The possibility of a corner solution, whence (6.16) becomes an inequality, leads to the possibility that individuals can have double-peaked preferences over the tax rate. They may prefer lower tax rates over a range, but after t exceeds some level they may stop working and therefore prefer yet higher tax rates imposed on others who are still working.

The effect on utility of a small change in the tax structure can be examined by totally differentiating U with respect to a and t. Hence, starting from the total differential:

$$dU = U_c dc + U_y dy \tag{6.17}$$

and using the rule that:

$$dc = \frac{\partial c}{\partial a} da + \frac{\partial c}{\partial t} dt + \frac{\partial c}{\partial y} dy \tag{6.18}$$

appropriate substitution of (6.18) into (6.17) and rearranging gives

$$dU = dy\{U_c(1 - t) + U_y\} + U_c(da - y dt). \tag{6.19}$$

But from the first-order condition in (6.16), the term in curly brackets in (6.19) is zero, so that

$$dU = U_c(da - ydt).$$ (6.20)

This is Roberts's result (1977, p. 332). Differentiation of (6.4) gives:

$$\frac{da}{dt} = \bar{y} + t\frac{d\bar{y}}{dt}$$ (6.21)

where the second term, which is typically negative, reflects the effect of increasing the tax rate on labour supply in aggregate. Rewriting (6.20) by dividing by dt, and using (6.21) to substitute for the resulting da/dt, gives:

$$\frac{dU}{dt} = U_c(\bar{y} + \frac{td\bar{y}}{dt} - y).$$ (6.22)

This modifies the result of section 6.1, and shows that some individuals with $y < \bar{y}$ will not vote for an increase in the tax rate.

Hierarchical Adherence

The above framework used by Roberts to establish Lemma 1 shows how the assumption that the ranking of individuals is not affected by the tax system implies a clear set of preferences over tax schedules. This can be seen by considering persons i and j, for whom $y_j \geq y_i$ whatever the tax structure; the natural ordering of individuals is always such that $j > i$. From equation (6.20), j's change in utility as a result of an increase in t is given by:

$$\frac{dU_j}{dt} = U_c^j \left\{ \frac{da}{dt} - y_j \right\}$$ (6.23)

where U_c^j is $\partial U_j / \partial c$ and of course y_j is a function of a and t. If the other individual, i, is indifferent between the two tax rates, then dU_i/d$t = 0$ and da/d$t = y_i$. Substituting for this value of da/dt into equation (6.23) gives:

$$\frac{dU_j}{dt} = U_c^j(y_i - y_j).$$ (6.24)

By assumption, $y_j \geq y_i$, for $j > i$ so that with person i indifferent, person j is necessarily worse off as a result of the increase in the tax rate. If, alternatively, person j is indifferent, then i is better off from an increase in t. So long as the ranking of individuals by income is unchanged, it can also be seen that if an individual prefers a lower to a higher rate tax, all those with a higher income prefer a lower rate. Furthermore, if an individual prefers a higher rate, all those with a lower income also prefer a higher rate.

Hierarchical adherence thus guarantees a set of preferences that generates a stable majority associated with the median voter's preferences and, as Roberts (1977, p.337) shows, quasi-transitive social choices under a broader class of choice mechanisms. These results are, as suggested earlier, intuitively quite transparent and extremely strong, especially as hierarchical adherence appears to be a fairly weak restriction on individuals' preferences. The argument can easily be extended to the case of the tax function with a tax-free threshold and is therefore not rehearsed here. The question nevertheless arises of whether the result can be applied more widely. This question is examined in the following section.

6.3   A TWO-PERIOD MODEL

This section establishes the validity of Roberts's Lemma 1 in a simple two-period model with a linear income tax and shows that it fails to hold in a two-period model with an income tax having a tax-free threshold.

Income Determination

The assumption of hierarchical adherence will be preserved simply by ignoring conventional labour supply decisions and assuming an exogenously given distribution of income-earning ability, y. However, the tax parameters affect individuals' decisions regarding the distribution of taxable income across their lifetime using a simple version of the higher education model examined elsewhere in this book. Suppose that individuals must choose between working in both periods and earning y in each period, or investing in higher education and bearing a fixed cost, c, as well as forgoing current earnings of $(1-h)y$, where $0 < h < 1$, in return for higher second-period earnings, ky, where $k > 1$. This simple framework has been chosen for purposes of exposition. It is much more specialized than required; in general the results obtained below only require that taxable income can be transferred through the lifetime and that individuals of higher income-earning ability face lower costs of transferring income across periods.

Assume also a one-to-one correspondence between utility and post tax income, z, given by $z(a, t, y)$. Therefore for an equivalent form of Lemma 1 to hold it is necessary to demonstrate that along indifference curves, $dt/da|_{z_i} \geq dt/da|_{z_j}$ for $i < j$. As pre-tax income is assumed to be monotonically increasing in y this implies:

$$d(dt/da|_z)/dy \leq 0. \tag{6.25}$$

Thus Lemma 1 will hold in this framework if the slope of each individual's indifference curve falls with income-earning ability. The following sub-sections examine the condition in (6.25) for two types of tax schedule.

A Linear Income Tax

Under the linear income tax, uneducated individuals receive a post-tax and transfer income in each period of $z_1^u = z_2^u = y + a - yt$. Ignoring discounting, net lifetime income, Z^u, is therefore:

$$Z^u = 2\{a + y(1 - t)\}. \tag{6.26}$$

Assuming for the moment that education expenses are non-deductible, an individual who invests in higher education receives $z_1^e = hy(1 - t) + a - c$ and $z_2^e = ky(1 - t) + a$ in periods 1 and 2 respectively. Net lifetime income is therefore:

$$Z^e = y(h + k)(1 - t) + 2a - c. \tag{6.27}$$

Given income-earning ability, y_i, an individual will choose education if $Z^e > Z^u$, that is, if:

$$y_i(1 - t)\{(h + k) - 2\} - c > 0. \tag{6.28}$$

It can be seen from equation (6.28) that for a strictly positive proportion of the population to be educated it is necessary to have:

$$h + k > 2. \tag{6.29}$$

Denote by y^* the level of ability above which individuals become educated (the educational choice margin familiar from earlier chapters). Using (6.26) and (6.27) it is possible to determine the slope of indifference curves in (a, t) space. Assuming that $y > a$, for an uneducated individual, (6.26) shows that:

$$dt/da|_z = 1/y \tag{6.30}$$

therefore

$$d(dt/d\alpha|_z)/dy = -1/y^2 < 0 \qquad \text{for } y \leq y^*. \tag{6.31}$$

From (6.27) the slope of an indifference curve for an educated individual is:

$$dt/d\alpha|_z = 2/\{y(h+k)\} \tag{6.32}$$

so that:

$$d(dt/d\alpha|_z)/dy = -2/y^2(h+k) \leq 0 \qquad \text{for } y > y^*. \tag{6.33}$$

Loosely, (6.31) shows that the marginal tax rate preferred by uneducated individuals falls with ability level. Similarly (6.33) shows that the marginal tax rate preferred by educated individuals also falls with ability level. These results demonstrate that when considering an increase in t and α which leaves utility unchanged, the preferred level of progression falls with ability *within* each sub-group of educated or uneducated individuals. However, for (6.25) to hold it is necessary to demonstrate that indifference curves are downward-sloping over the whole range of y. Since educational choice, determined by (6.28), is a function of t it is necessary to consider the preferences of individuals whose educational status changes with changes in the tax structure. This introduces a discontinuity in the schedules at the choice margin, y^*, requiring analysis of a discrete change at that point. Hence $dt/d\alpha|_z$ should be as shown in schedule (i) of Figure 6.3. Comparing the left- and right-hand-side derivatives at y^*, for (6.25) to hold it is necessary that $\lim_{y\uparrow y^*} dt/d\alpha|_z > \lim_{y\downarrow y^*} dt/d\alpha|_z$, which from (6.30) and (6.32) implies $1/y > 2/[y(h+k)]$ and therefore that $h+k > 2$. This must be true from equation (6.28); therefore (6.25) must hold for all y and Roberts's Lemma 1 applies.

A Tax-free Threshold

Assume that all individuals are taxed at the rate, t, above a tax-free amount, a, which is less than the minimum value of y. Net income for an uneducated individual in each period is therefore $z_1^u = z_2^u = y - (y-a)t$. For those above y^*, and if the cost of education is tax-deductible, post-tax income in the first period is given by:

$$z_1^e = hy - c - (hy - c - a)t \qquad \text{for } hy - c > a \tag{6.34}$$

$$= hy - c \qquad \text{for } hy - c < a. \tag{6.35}$$

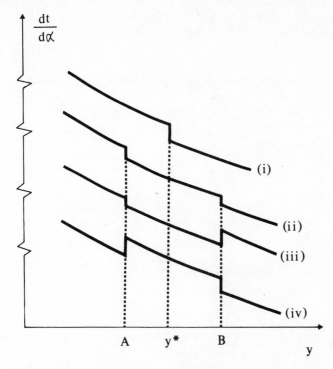

Figure 6.3   Tax preferences and income in a two-period model

This assumes that if the cost is not tax-deductible, post-tax income is given by:

$$z_1^e = hy - c(hy - a)t \qquad \text{for } hy > a \qquad (6.36)$$

$$= hy - c \qquad\qquad \text{for } hy < a. \qquad (6.37)$$

Proceeding as before with the assumption that the cost of education is not tax-deductible, income in the second period for all educated individuals is:

$$z_2^e = ky - (ky - a)t. \qquad (6.38)$$

For an uneducated person, net lifetime income, Z^u, is $2\{y - (y - a)t\}$, so that along an indifference curve:

$$dt/da = t/(y - a). \qquad (6.39)$$

For an educated individual with first-period taxable income below the exemption, lifetime income, Z^e, is $hy - c + ky - (ky - a)t$, so that along an indifference curve:

$$dt/da = t/(ky - a). \tag{6.40}$$

For an educated person with first-period income above the tax-free threshold, a, net lifetime income, Z^e, is $hy - c - (hy - a)t + ky - (ky - a)t$, so that along an indifference curve:

$$dt/da = 2t/\{(h + k)y - 2a\}. \tag{6.41}$$

Consider the sub-groups in turn. For the uneducated, from (6.39):

$$d(dt/da)/dy = - t/(y - a)^2 < 0. \tag{6.42}$$

For the educated below the exemption in the first period, from (6.40):

$$d(dt/da)/dy = - kt/(ky - a)^2 < 0. \tag{6.43}$$

For the educated above the exemption in the first period, from (6.41):

$$d(dt/da)/dy = - 2(h + k)/\{(h + k)y - 2a\}^2 < 0. \tag{6.44}$$

Consequently condition (6.25) is satisfied within sub-groups but it is again necessary to check the slopes of the function at any discontinuity. In this case there are two points of discontinuity, labelled A and B in Figure 6.3. Point A is the discontinuity due to the educational choice decision and B is that caused by the tax-free threshold. Lemma 1 holds for schedule (ii) of Figure 6.3. Lemma 1 will be violated if either of the situations depicted in schedules (iii) or (iv) of Figure 6.3 occur. For (6.25) to hold at A it is necessary that $\lim_{y\uparrow y*} dt/da|_z > \lim_{y\downarrow y*} dt/da|_z$, from (6.39) and (6.40) this implies $t/(y - a) > t/(ky - a)$ and therefore that $k > 1$, which holds by assumption.

Consider discontinuity B: for (6.25) to hold it is necessary that $\lim_{hy\uparrow a} dt/da|_z > \lim_{hy\downarrow a} dt/da|_z$, from (6.40) and (6.41) this implies $t/(ky - a) > 2t/(h + k)y - 2a$ which requires that $h > k$. This can never be true, thus condition (6.25) is violated. Individuals of higher income-earning ability who are educated and above the threshold in the first period will prefer a tax and threshold combination (a, t) with a higher marginal tax rate than that preferred by someone who is also educated but has marginally lower income-earning ability and is therefore below the threshold in the first period. If the cost of education is tax-deductible, it can be shown that for (6.25) to hold it is necessary that $c < (h-k)y$, which can also never be true.

This result has a straightforward intuitive explanation. For utility to remain constant, an increase in the threshold requires an increase in t of, say, Δt. For individuals who are educated but below the threshold in the first period, an increase in the threshold benefits them only in the second period, by an amount $t\Delta a$. In the second period the effect of a rise in t reduces income by $(ky-a)\Delta t$. In comparison, an individual of slightly higher income-earning ability who is educated, but whose income is above the threshold in both periods, benefits by an amount $t\Delta a$ in both periods. However, in the first period the tax increase only imposes a cost of $(hy-a)\Delta t$, which is smaller than the second-period cost of $(ky-a)\Delta t$. Thus for a given increase in the threshold, the higher-ability individual above the threshold obtains twice the benefit, but pays less than twice the cost of the tax change. Thus the individual with higher income-earning ability may favour a higher marginal tax rate and Lemma 1 is violated.

7.   Transfer payments, means-testing and inequality

There has been a large, though still inconclusive, debate on the effects of higher education on income distribution. Some of the literature was discussed in Chapter 2, where it was seen that although higher education provides a clear example of the need to consider lifetime redistribution, since the tax effects are felt over the whole of the working life and the educational choice decision itself is based on lifetime considerations, studies often restrict attention to annual incomes. The majority of a cohort, by supporting a tax-financed grant, are seen to be supporting a policy which increases the inequality of net lifetime income; although the incomes of the uneducated are increased, those of the people above the educational choice margin increase by relatively more. The grants are therefore essentially regressive.

This aspect was also discussed in Chapter 5 when considering the maximization of a social welfare function with a trade-off between equity and efficiency, with both proportional and progressive income taxation. The present chapter focuses on inequality in the context of a proportional income tax and majority voting. However, additional complications are introduced in the form of transfer payments to the poor and means-testing of the higher education grant.

In order to provide a basic point of comparison with later results, Table 7.1 illustrates the inequality-increasing effect of a grant in the case of the proportional tax of Chapter 4. The parameter values on which Table 7.1 is based are given in the notes to the table. The inequality measures reported are respectively the coefficient of variation, η, the variance of logarithms, σ^2, and Atkinson's inequality measure $I(1.6)$ of net lifetime income (with a relative inequality aversion coefficient of 1.6). The inequality measures cannot of course be calculated using explicit formulae. They are based on a simulated cohort consisting of 15,000 individuals, after solving for the endogenous variables using the method presented in Chapter 4.

The present chapter also introduces social transfers whereby those with pre-tax incomes below some threshold level are brought up to a minimum income level. An obvious effect of such transfers is to reduce inequality generally, but if the threshold (pre-tax) income level is fixed in real terms

118

Table 7.1   Majority voting and inequality

	Majority choice	No grant
ρ	0.35	0
p	0.148	0.105
t	0.299	0.294
η	0.704	0.688
σ^2	0.280	0.269
I(1.6)	0.210	0.203

Notes:
$\delta = 0.7$; $r = 0.6$, $R = 6.0$; $h = 0.2$; $u = 0.1$.
The cost of education is given by $c = d_1(p + \theta)^{-d_2}$ with $d_1 = 2.6$; $d_2 = 0.3$; $\theta = 0.1$.
Median value of $y = 10$; coefficient of variation of $y = 0.5$.

then any general growth in incomes will reduce the number of people below the threshold. This implies, first, that the majority will support, *ceteris paribus*, a larger grant and, secondly, any increase in the grant is associated with a slightly larger increase in lifetime inequality than formerly. Transfers are introduced in section 7.1.

It has been noted above that intra-marginal individuals would not be influenced in their educational choice decision by small changes in the grant. This suggests that a 'cheaper' method of inducing more people to invest in higher education (which is the only way in this model for the non-educated to obtain a rising income profile) is to concentrate the grant on those near the educational choice margin. Such a concentration reduces both the costs of a grant and the extent to which inequality increases. The effect of introducing a form of means-testing into the grant system, whereby the grant is progressively reduced as income increases beyond a specified level, is also examined. By reducing the total cost of the grant, the majority are thereby prepared to support a higher basic grant. The taper does not affect the educational choice decision of intra-marginal individuals. This policy also has the effect of reducing the extent to which inequality increases when the basic grant is increased. Means-testing of the grant is introduced in section 7.2. Numerical comparisons between alternative schemes are finally reported in section 7.3

7.1   THE INTRODUCTION OF SOCIAL TRANSFERS

Suppose the transfer system is the guaranteed minimum income variety, such that it raises the net incomes of those with a pre-tax income below a specified level, m, to the level $(1-t)m$. The value of $(1-t)m$ may be regarded as a poverty level. Hence all those below m receive the same after-tax-and-transfer income as an individual with a pre-tax income of m. If m remains constant in real terms, the effect of a general growth of earnings (which results from a higher proportion of the cohort investing in higher education) is to reduce the number of individuals below m. The consequent reduction in the total amount of transfer payments compensates to some extent for the higher cost of financing higher education as ρ is increased. The choice of ρ by all those below y^* therefore increases. The question arises, however, of whether it is appropriate to regard the guaranteed minimum income as being fixed in real or relative terms. In practice the choice depends on value judgements regarding poverty; there is no 'correct' definition. However, many governments in recent years have moved away from earnings-related benefits and the indexation of transfers according to average earnings, towards a more absolute view using a price index.

For those with $y \leq m$, the amount of the transfer is equal to $(1-t)(m-y)$. Hence in the first period the total amount required to finance transfer payments is equal to the size of the cohort multiplied by:

$$(1-t)\int_0^m (m-y)\mathrm{d}F(y). \tag{7.1}$$

This expression can be simplified to:

$$(1-t)\{m\mathrm{F}(m)-\bar{y}\,\mathrm{F}_1(m)\} \tag{7.2}$$

where $\mathrm{F}_1(m)$ denotes the proportion of total income obtained by those with incomes below m. This is again the incomplete first-moment distribution introduced in Chapter 4. The first term in (7.2), after multiplying by the size of the cohort, is the amount that would need to be given to those below m in order to bring them up to $(1-t)m$, if they had no income. The second term reflects the total amount of income, after paying tax at the rate t, obtained by those with $y<m$. The difference between the two terms therefore measures the total *net* transfers required.

In the second period all incomes are increased because of the external benefit of higher education, by a proportion g. As those below the threshold, m, obviously would not invest in higher education, the amount needed to finance transfers in the second period is:

$$(1-t)\{m\mathrm{F}(m)-\bar{y}(1+g)\mathrm{F}_1(m)\}. \tag{7.3}$$

The present value of the total amount of income tax raised is precisely the same as in the model in Chapter 4, and given by equation (4.19). It is convenient to write this as tC. Rewrite (7.2) as $(1-t)A$ and (7.3) as $(1-t)B$, then the new budget constraint facing the government is:

$$(1-t)\left(A+\frac{B}{1+r}\right)+R_t=tC$$

thus

$$t=\frac{A+B/(1+r)+R_t}{A+B/(1+r)+C}. \tag{7.4}$$

The determination of the educational choice margin is unchanged, and is given by the positive root of equation (4.5).

A major implication of transfer payments for the analysis of inequality is that the population must be divided into four groups, rather than just two groups of those above and below the educational choice margin. Net lifetime income, V, is given by:

$$\begin{aligned}V=(1-h)(1-t)y-c(1-\rho)\\ +y(1+s+g)(1-t)/(1+r)\end{aligned} \qquad \text{for } y>y^* \tag{7.5}$$

$$V=(1-t)y+y(1+g)(1-t)/(1+r) \qquad \text{for } m<y<y^* \tag{7.6}$$

$$V=(1-t)m+(1-t)(1+g)y/(1+r) \qquad \text{for } (1+g)y>m>y \tag{7.7}$$

$$V=(1-t)m\{1+1/(1+r)\} \qquad \text{for } m>(1+g)y \tag{7.8}$$

Equation (7.7) corresponds to the case where an individual below the educational choice margin receives the transfer in only the first period, while (7.8) applies to an individual receiving a transfer in both periods.

7.2   MEANS-TESTING OF THE GRANT

Each person above the educational choice margin has been assumed to receive a grant of ρc towards the cost of education. This means that some individuals receive a larger grant than is necessary to induce them to invest in education. Suppose, however, that a 'taper' is introduced such that only those at the margin receive the full grant, which is reduced progressively for $y>y^*$. Assume that the grant, $H(y)$ is determined according to:

$$H(y)=\rho c-\gamma(y-y^*) \qquad \text{for } y^*\leq y\leq y^*+\rho c/\gamma=y_u \tag{7.9}$$

$$=0 \qquad \text{for } y>y_u.$$

Table 7.2 Majority voting with means-testing and social transfers

m	6		8		0		6		8		0	
γ	0		0		0.2		0.2		0.3		0.3	
ρ	0.4	0	0.55	0	0.65	0	0.7	0	0.9	0	0.8	0
p	0.155	0.104	0.178	0.101	0.203	0.105	0.213	0.104	0.266	0.101	0.239	0.105
t	0.308	0.303	0.332	0.326	0.299	0.294	0.308	0.303	0.330	0.326	0.300	0.294
η	0.683	0.665	0.641	0.616	0.694	0.688	0.671	0.665	0.619	0.616	0.691	0.688
σ^2	0.229	0.217	0.179	0.162	0.282	0.269	0.229	0.217	0.175	0.162	0.281	0.269
I(1.6)	0.180	0.171	0.148	0.135	0.210	0.203	0.179	0.171	0.143	0.135	0.210	0.203

Note: $\delta = 0.7$; $u = 0.1$; $h = 0.2$; $R = 6.0$; $r = 0.6$; $d_1 = 2.6$; $d_2 = 0.3$; $\theta = 0.1$.

The educational choice margin, y^*, may be determined in the usual way. As long as y_u is sufficiently large, all those above y^* have an incentive to become educated despite the reduction in their grant. The cost per member of the cohort of financing any given value of ρ is no longer $\rho c\{1 - F(y^*)\}$, but is reduced to:

$$\int_{y^*}^{y_u} \{\rho c - \gamma(y - y^*)\} dF(y).$$ (7.10)

This expression may be rearranged to give:

$$\rho c\{F(y_u) - F(y^*)\} - \gamma \bar{y}[\{F_1(y_u) - F_1(y^*)\} - (y^*/\bar{y})\{F(y_u) - F(y^*)\}].$$ (7.11)

The deficit neutrality condition, (7.4), can therefore be modified simply by altering the expression for R_t. The examination of lifetime inequality now requires additional consideration of the separate group having $y > y_u$, whose members receive no grant. The lifetime income of those with $y^* < y < y_u$ is reduced by an amount equal to $\gamma(y - y^*)$. These analytical results, along with those of section 7.1, can be used to compare alternative policies. Having obtained results, based on the iterative search procedure described in Chapter 4, the inequality measures can then be calculated for a simulated distribution of individuals. As mentioned above, a population of 15,000 individuals is used in each case below.

7.3 HIGHER EDUCATION AND INEQUALITY

Some Comparisons

In this section the precise effects of introducing a minimum income guarantee and the tapering of the grant are examined using numerical examples. The effects on both the majority choice of ρ and the inequality of net lifetime income are considered, where the parameters of the model are otherwise the same as in Table 7.1. A summary of the alternative results is given in Table 7.2. For each specification, the table reports alternative inequality measures along with the tax rate and the proportion educated, for both $\rho = 0$ and that value of ρ which maximizes the net lifetime income of all those below y^*.

It can be seen that the introduction of a minimum income guarantee raises the preferred value of ρ of those who do not invest in higher education, as shown by the first two cases in Table 7.2. The values of m used

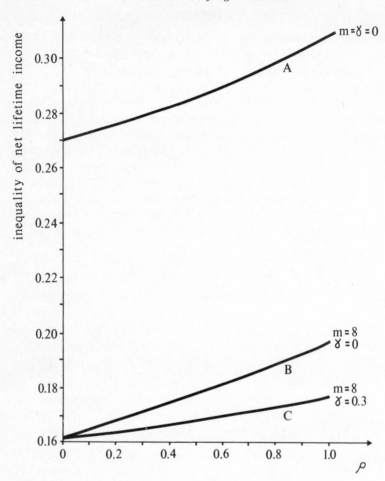

Figure 7.1   Lifetime inequality and the grant

in Table 7.2 may be judged in comparison with the median value of y, of 10 units. Since the proportional increase in earnings determined by the external effect of $g(p)$ reduces the number of those with incomes below m in the second period, the marginal cost to those below y^* of increasing ρ is reduced. The marginal benefit, for given p, is unchanged, so that the preferred value of ρ is higher. This result follows despite the fact that the tax rate is higher than where there is no guaranteed minimum income. This is because it is the marginal tax cost of raising the grant which is relevant, not the absolute value of the tax rate. Increasing ρ raises the proportion above the educational choice margin, which increases inequality for any given value of m. However, the effect of the minimum income guarantee means that inequality is lower, for any given value of ρ. From Table 7.2, an increase in the threshold income level for transfers, from 6 to 8, raises the majority choice of ρ from 0.4 to 0.55 and the proportion investing in higher education from 0.155 to 0.178, but the effect on inequality is more than offset by the inequality-reducing effect of the larger amount of social transfers.

Means-testing of the education grant does not affect the marginal benefit to those below y^* of increasing ρ. However, the marginal cost of increasing ρ falls. This leads to support for a higher value of ρ, a greater proportion investing in higher education and therefore an increase in inequality. However, the effect on inequality of increasing the value of ρ is not as great as in the basic model. Table 7.2 shows that the introduction of tapering the grant leads to a much higher preferred value of ρ and reduces the inequality measures.

Further information about the effect on lifetime inequality of varying ρ is given in Figure 7.1. This shows the variation in the variance of logarithms of net lifetime income for three cases: the basic model, the case where $m = 8$, and where $m = 8$ is combined with $\gamma = 0.3$. This shows the large effect of the guaranteed minimum income in reducing inequality for all levels of ρ. However, the existence of transfer payments means that inequality increases slightly more rapidly with ρ than in the basic case. This is slightly reversed when the grant taper is introduced.

A Zero External Effect

In the basic model, an external effect of higher education is a necessary, though not a sufficient, condition for uneducated individuals to gain from the tax-financed grant towards the cost of higher education. This is because the introduction of a grant requires an increase in the tax rate, though this is mitigated to some extent by the tax base effect of higher education in raising incomes. Results for a means-tested grant ($\gamma > 0$) and the complete absence of an external effect ($\delta = 0$) are, however, shown in Table 7.3. In this case it can be seen that the cost of introducing a small grant is sufficiently reduced so that the tax-base effect of the private returns to higher education is sufficient to reduce the tax rate. With γ of 0.2 and 0.3 respectively, those below y^* have maximum net lifetime income when 10 per cent and 15 per cent of the cost of higher education per person (at the educational choice margin) is financed by taxation. The effect of increasing ρ on the tax base may itself be regarded as an external effect of higher education, since only the net-of-tax returns are appropriated by individual investors.

Table 7.3 Majority voting with no external effect

	$\gamma=0.2$ Majority choice	$\rho=0$	$\gamma=0.3$ Majority choice	$\rho=0$
ρ	0.1	0	0.15	0
p	0.115	0.104	0.12	0.104
t	0.300	0.301	0.300	0.301
c	4.122	4.185	4.089	4.185
η	0.693	0.693	0.694	0.693
σ^2	0.271	0.270	0.271	0.270
I(1.6)	0.204	0.203	0.204	0.203

Note: $\delta=0$; $m=0$; other parameters are as in Tables 7.1 and 7.2.

Further Comparisons

Table 7.4 presents results which show the change in ρ caused by changes in both the minimum income guarantee and the degree to which the grant is means-tested. As above, γ denotes the rate of taper in the means-testing of the grant, and the minimum-income guarantee is operated such that all those with gross incomes below m have their net income increased to the post-tax value of m, that is $(1-t)m$. The variance of logarithms of the basic distribution of ability is denoted by σ^2. Table 7.4 gives two columns for each set of parameter values. The first applies to the counter-factual situation in which there is no grant, while the second column refers to the value of ρ preferred by the majority of members of the cohort.

Table 7.4 Inequality and the level of grant

	Example 1 $\sigma^2=0.223$ $\gamma=0$ $m=0$		Example 2 $\sigma^2=0.223$ $\gamma=0$ $m=6$		Example 3 $\sigma^2=0.223$ $\gamma=0.4$ $m=0$		Example 4 $\sigma^2=0.243$ $\gamma=0.3$ $m=0$	
ρ	0	0.35	0	0.40	0	0.90	0	0.75
t	0.294	0.299	0.303	0.308	0.294	0.300	0.286	0.291
p	0.105	0.148	0.104	0.154	0.105	0.268	0.118	0.237
c	4.18	3.95	4.19	3.92	4.18	3.95	4.11	3.60
I(1.6)	0.203	0.210	0.171	0.180	0.203	0.208	0.203	0.210

Note: The cost of education per student is given by $c=2.6\,(p+0.1)^{-0.3}$. The above results were obtained for the following parameter values: $r=0.6$, $R=6$, $h=0.2$, $u=0.1$, $\delta=0.7$.

A rise in the minimum income guarantee induces a rise in the grant. This is explained by considering two changes. First, providing a guaranteed minimum income raises the tax rate, t, required to support government expenditure and reduces the proportion educated, p. As additional growth generated by the proportion educated is assumed to be marginally diminishing, a fall in the proportion educated ensures that the external benefit from inducing the marginal person to invest in education rises. The combined effect of these two factors is seen to raise the median voter's preferred level of the grant; this is seen by comparing the preferred value of ρ for examples 1 and 2 in Table 7.4.

Means-testing benefits will also raise the median voter's desired level of the grant. With means-testing, the tax rate required to support a given grant falls and therefore the proportion educated for that level of grant rises. Thus the marginal benefit to the majority of inducing another person to invest in higher education falls. However, the marginal cost to the majority will also fall as, with the means-testing of benefits, inducing the marginal person to invest in higher education costs relatively less. The relative magnitude of these effects, which will depend upon both the concavity of the external growth function and the degree of means-testing, determines whether the grant rises with increased means-testing. It is shown in Table 7.4, by comparing the preferred level of the grant in examples 1 and 3, that the net effect of means-testing is to raise the level of funding the majority is prepared to support.

Inequality and the Level of the Grant

It is necessary to consider the two effects on inequality which stem from a change in conditions. The first is the direct effect on inequality of a change in either the minimum-income guarantee or the extent to which the grant is means-tested, while the second is the effect on inequality of the induced change in the level of funding accompanying the initial change. The net result will determine the overall effect of a change on the dispersion of incomes.

The measure of inequality reported is Atkinson's measure, based on an inequality aversion parameter of 1.6. A range of inequality measures was found to give similar results.

A rise in the minimum-income guarantee leads directly to a fall in dispersion for a given grant as all members of the population below the guaranteed minimum income have their incomes raised. However, as shown in the previous section, this leads to an increase in the grant which counteracts the direct effect. Comparison of these two effects, as presented by the measures of inequality in Table 7.4, shows that Atkinson's measure of inequality falls from 0.210 to 0.180 whilst the median voter's preferred level of funding rises from 0.35 to 0.40. This can be explained by referring to Figure 7.1. Schedule A shows the relationship between measured inequality and the level of the grant for the case of no means-testing and no minimum-income guarantee. Schedule B, which lies below schedule A, shows the same relationship when there is a minimum-income guarantee. With the grant initially at 0.35, Atkinson's measure is shown by schedule A. However a rise in ρ to 0.4, which occurs as a result of the introduction of a minimum-income gurantee, yields an inequality measure shown by the lower schedule B. Thus the downward shift in the schedule means that a rise in the minimum-income guarantee leads to a fall in inequality, despite the endogenous rise in the level of the grant.

Means-testing of benefit can also be viewed in terms of its direct and indirect effects on the dispersion of incomes. The direct effect reduces the dispersion, as high-income individuals receive a progressively smaller grant. However, the indirect effect of an induced rise in funding causes a rise in dispersion. The inequality measures in examples 1 and 3 in Table 7.4 show the relative magnitude of these effects. It is seen that, despite the large induced rise in the grant, inequality in the distribution of net lifetime income falls. This can again be explained by referring to Figure 7.1. Schedule C shows the relationship between inequality and the grant where the grant is means-tested. Means-testing serves to flatten the schedule considerably, so that a rise in funding leads to smaller increase in the dispersion of incomes. This ensures that even the considerably large increase in ρ to 0.90 yields less dispersion than when the grant is not means-tested, even with ρ zero. Thus a higher grant is again associated with a lower dispersion of the distribution of net lifetime income.

In reality it is possible that more than one factor may change at a time. The difficulties presented by this can again be shown by referring to Table 7.4. Example 4 presents results when both the initial dispersion of income-earning ability and the degree to which the grant is means-tested are simultaneously varied. In this situation, while both factors lead to an increase in the grant, they affect the dispersion of incomes in conflicting ways and in total lead to an unaltered dispersion of incomes. A partial analysis may have concluded in this situation that tax-financed grants for higher education are neutral in their effect on the dispersion of incomes.

8.   The use of a tax surcharge

Throughout this book the concept of a deferred fee, arising from the higher taxes which must be paid over the working life, has played a major role. Any grant or other subsidy made available to those who invest in higher education must be financed by an increase in taxation. Given that those who invest have relatively high incomes, the overall increase in inequality arising from the grant depends partly on the progressivity of the income tax structure. One way of making the deferred fee element of grants explicit, and at the same time having a subsidy scheme which avoids some of the regressivity inherent in a simple grant scheme, is to have a tax surcharge. This takes the form of an addition to the tax rate paid during the working life by those who invest in higher education. It is only partially equivalent to an income-contingent loan scheme. Some individuals may never effectively 'repay' their grant from the higher taxes, while it is possible for very high-income recipients to pay more through the tax surcharge (combined with the deferred-fee element through the general equilibrium effect) than the grant or 'loan' received. As explained earlier, the same is also true of a standard grant system in which the deferred fee itself may exceed the grant. But the large majority would not fully repay the grant under appropriate choice of the tax surcharge.

This chapter therefore modifies the model used in previous chapters in order to focus on the implications of using a tax surcharge, in combination with a proportional income tax system, to finance a higher education grant. The government's budget constraint is handled explicitly and the level of the grant is determined endogenously using a public-choice framework. It would of course be possible to use the framework to examine the maximization of a social welfare function, following the approach of Chapter 5, but this would not introduce any new principles and is therefore omitted here. The model is used to examine the implications for the distribution of individual rates of return, rather than focusing on an arbitrary single rate from the distribution. The redistributive effects of such a scheme, allowing for both direct and indirect effects, are also considered. Hence, the endogenously determined level of the grant is used to analyse the following questions. First, what is the effect of the introduction of a tax surcharge on the proportion of the population enrolling in higher education? Secondly, what is the effect of a tax surcharge on income inequality? The basic model is modified to allow for a surcharge in section 8.1. The distribution of rates of return to investment in higher education is examined in section 8.2. Some comparative static results are then presented in section 8.3. Finally, section 8.4 considers lifetime inequality.

8.1   MODIFICATIONS TO THE BASIC MODEL

The basic model used here is the same as that presented in Chapter 4, and is therefore described very briefly before introducing the tax surcharge. Attention is restricted to a single cohort of individuals, where the lifetime is divided into two periods of unequal length. During the first period, individuals may invest in higher education. The ith individual obtains y_i in the first period, if uneducated, but only a proportion hy_i if investing in higher education, with $0 < h < 1$. The variable y reflects both income earning ability and the ability to benefit from higher education, and is taken to be exogenous. No investment in education can take place during the second period. The private benefit of education is such that income in the second period of those who invest is increased by a proportion s_i to $y_i(1 + s_i)$. Those with higher income-earning ability are assumed to have a higher value of s, and for simplicity it is assumed that s_i is proportional to y_i, with $s_i = uy_i$.

In addition, *all* individuals benefit from an external effect of higher education in the form of productivity growth at the proportional rate, g, which arises as a result of the complementarity between skills. This externality depends on the proportion, p, of the cohort that invests in higher education, so that $g = g(p)$. Furthermore, suppose that the cost of education per person is fixed at the amount c. It might be argued that there are some economies of scale, so that c would fall as p, the proportion investing, rises. However, this type of effect has been examined in Appendix 4.2 and has been shown to have no influence on the relevant comparisons, so the · simpler assumption of fixed costs is retained.

The tax and transfer scheme is assumed to take the following form. There is an unconditional grant available to all those investing in higher education, and this can be expressed as a proportion, ρ, of the cost per person, c. Hence the value of the grant is ρc, and ρ is the policy variable which must be chosen by the government. Income taxation takes the simple form of a proportional tax imposed on all income at the rate, t. However, all those who invest in higher education must pay a tax surcharge of t' during their working lives, so that their effective tax rate is $t + t'$ in the second period. As explained above, the surcharge is only loosely related to a form of income-contingent loan. To the extent that the surcharge does not recover all the aggregate cost of the grant, the standard tax rate, t, must be higher than otherwise, and this imposes what has been called a deferred fee. The important components of the model are the educational choice and deficit neutrality schedules, and these are derived in the following subsections.

Educational Choice

Individuals' investment decisions are assumed to be based on the maximization of net lifetime income, given the various costs and returns from education. If r denotes the discount rate, the net present value of lifetime income of the ith individual who invests in higher education, V_i^E, is given by:

$$V_i^E = hy_i(1-t) - c(1-\rho) + y_i(1+s_i+g)(1-t-t')/(1+r). \qquad (8.1)$$

It is assumed here that individuals can borrow and lend as much as desired at the fixed interest rate, r. Hence there is no need to consider whether the net fee $c(1-\rho)$ is paid out of net income in the first period or is financed from borrowing, or some combination of the two.

For non-enrolled individuals, net lifetime income, V_i^N, is given by:

$$V_i^N = y_i(1-t) + y_i(1+g)(1-t)/(1+r). \qquad (8.2)$$

The value of y above which it is just worthwhile investing in higher education has been called the educational choice margin. It is found by equating (8.1) and (8.2) and solving for y. Substituting for $s_i = uy_i$ and rearranging, gives the following quadratic:

$$y^{*2}(1-t-t')u - y^*\{(1-t)(1-h)(1+r) + (1+g)t'\} - c(1-\rho)(1+r) = 0. \; (8.3)$$

It can be shown that this quadratic has only one feasible solution. All those with $y_i > y^*$ invest in higher education. In the simple case where the grant covers the whole direct cost of investing, and there is no surcharge, so that $t' = 0$ and $\rho = 1$, the value of y^* is equal to $(1-h)(1+r)/u$ and is independent of the proportional tax rate t. But in general (8.3) is complicated by the fact that with $t' \neq 0$ the coefficient on y^*, that is the term in curly brackets, contains the term g arising from the external effects. This has a major implication for solving (8.3) since g has been assumed to depend on the proportion of the cohort investing in higher education, which itself depends on the educational choice margin and the form of the distribution function of y, which influences the proportion of people above y^*. If $F(y)$ is the distribution function, so that $F(y)$ represents the proportion of the cohort with income-earning ability less than or equal to y, then p is equal to

$1 - F(y^*)$. Hence y^* is not in fact simply the root of a quadratic because y^* influences g. This contrasts with the simple proportional tax with no surcharge of Chapter 4, where the external effect does not enter the calculation of the educational choice margin.

It may be thought that (8.3) could be rewritten to express t in terms of the other variables, including y^*, but this approach is not available as there is no unique relationship between t and y^*. However, the model can be solved using an iterative numerical procedure described below. At each iteration, (8.3) is solved for a given value of g (taken from the previous iteration), and the method ensures that at the final stage, the value of y^* used to calculate $g(p)$ is precisely the same as the value of y^* given from the root of (8.3) for that value of g.

Deficit Neutrality

The government must decide on the value of ρ which determines the level of the grant, for a given tax surcharge, subject to its budget constraint. This introduces the dual-decision feature which is central to public finance issues: the government's decision variable itself influences the constraints facing individuals in their own decision-taking. Some of the variables which enter the government's constraint are in turn affected by the decisions of individuals in making their educational choices. Hence there must be mutual consistency between the decisions of the government and all individuals who are acting independently. In addition to the grant, the government must also raise sufficient income taxation to finance expenditure of R per member of the cohort, where R is regarded as a present value of expenditure over the life of the cohort.

The government's deficit neutrality constraint requires that the present value of tax revenue obtained from the cohort is equal to the amount required to finance R per person and the total grant payments. Since grants are paid in the first period, the total cost of the grant is equal to ρc multiplied by the number of people who receive it. If there are N people in the cohort, the cost is equal to ρcNp. Hence total government expenditure per member of the cohort, remembering that $p = 1 - F(y^*)$, is equal to:

$$R + \rho c\{1 - F(y^*)\}. \tag{8.4}$$

In view of the proportionality of the tax system, the calculation of tax revenue requires only an expression for the total income of each group. Let $\bar{y}$ denote the arithmetic mean value of y and let $F_1(y^*)$ denote the proportion of total income obtained by those with $y \leq y^*$ (that is, those below the educational choice margin). The total income of those *not* investing in higher education during the first period is thus equal to $N\bar{y}F_1(y^*)$. In the second period this total is simply increased by the growth term, g. Hence the tax revenue generated by those who do not invest in higher education is equal to:

$$tN\bar{y}F_1(y^*)\left\{1+\frac{1+g}{1+r}\right\}. \tag{8.5}$$

The total income of those who invest in higher education, during the first period when they forgo a proportion of income, is N multiplied by:

$$h\bar{y}\{1-F_1(y^*)\}. \tag{8.6}$$

The total second-period income of those who invest in higher education is more complex. From equation (8.1), the second-period income of the ith educated person is $y_i(1+uy_i+g)$, so it is necessary to handle a sum of squared values of y. The derivation is not given here because it is presented in Appendix 4.1, where it is shown that total income can be expressed as N multiplied by:

$$\bar{y}\left[(1+g)\{1-F_1(y^*)\}+u\bar{y}(1+\eta_y^2)\{1-F_2(y^*)\}\right] \tag{8.7}$$

where η_y is the coefficient of variation of y and $F_2(y^*)$ is equal to $\int_0^{y^*}y^2dF(y)/\int_0^\infty y^2dF(y)$. The total tax revenue obtained from those who invest in higher education is therefore Nt multiplied by (8.6), plus $N(t+t')$ multiplied by the present value of (8.7). Denote the term in square brackets in (8.7) by Φ. The present value of tax revenue per capita from the cohort as a whole can be shown to be:

$$t\bar{y}\Omega+\bar{y}t'\Phi/(1+r) \tag{8.8}$$

where $\Omega=F_1(y^*)+\{(1+g)F_1(y^*)+\Phi\}/(1+r)+h\{1-F_1(y^*)\}. \tag{8.9}$

Equating the expenditure requirement (8.4) and the tax revenue (8.8) therefore gives the required deficit neutrality constraint:

$$t=\{(R/\bar{y})-t'\Phi/(1+r)\}/\Omega. \tag{8.10}$$

It remains to specify the form of $g(p)$. Previous chapters have made extensive use of a flexible functional form, involving a single parameter, δ, and which captures reasonable *a priori* assumptions, given by:

$$g(p) = \delta p/(1+p). \tag{8.11}$$

Thus when no one invests in higher education $p = 0$ and $g = 0$, and g approaches a maximum of $\delta/2$.

Solving the Model

The problem is to solve simultaneously the two non-linear equations (8.3) and (8.10), remembering that g is given by (8.11), in order to obtain values of t and y^* for given values of t', r, h, u, R and ρ. This cannot be achieved analytically because of the non-linearity of the model, but numerical solutions can be obtained using the following two-stage iterative procedure, which has been found to converge rapidly. In the first stage, the quadratic (8.3) is solved to obtain a value of y^*, say y_1^*, corresponding to an initial arbitrary value of t, say t_1. In the very first iteration the value of g is set arbitrarily, but in subsequent iterations it is based on the previous value of y^*. The second stage of each iteration involves solving (8.10) for the tax rate, say t_2, given the value of y^*, y_1^*, obtained from the first stage. In this second stage g is calculated using y_1^*. The two tax rates are then compared. If $t_2 < t_1$ it is clear that y_1^* is too small and the value of t_1 is correspondingly too large. The value of t_1 is therefore reduced and the two-stage procedure repeated; alternatively if $t_1 < t_2$ then t_1 is increased. In this way convergence to a situation where $t_1 = t_2$ is achieved. This is a modification of the procedure described in Chapter 4. The calculations require an explicit assumption to be made about the distribution function $F(y)$. As in previous chapters, the calculations use the lognormal form.

Majority Voting

The following analysis concentrates on the assumption that the government sets that value of ρ which is supported by a simple majority of the cohort. Each individual is assumed to prefer that value of ρ which maximizes the net present value of lifetime income. For the use of a social welfare function, the approach described in Chapter 5 could easily be adopted if necessary.

The public-choice approach requires consideration of the question of whether or not a stable majority exists, given that some individuals will be expected to have double-peaked preferences. This is because some individuals who do not invest in higher education become worse off as the value of ρ increases beyond a certain level. But for some higher value of ρ it becomes worthwhile for those individuals to invest, so they then have a personal interest in voting for yet a higher value of ρ.

Despite such double-peaked preferences it has been shown in Chapter 4 that the model generates a stable majority in favour of a particular value of ρ. This is because, with proportional taxation, differentiation of equation (8.2) shows that all those below the educational choice margin share a common view about the desired value of ρ; that is, the value which maximizes their net lifetime income. Hence, so long as less then half the cohort invests in higher education, the (unanimous) preferences of the majority (those not investing) may be identified with those of the median individual in the distribution of y. Hence the procedure described above must be repeated for alternative values of ρ, and in each case the net lifetime income of the median individual is calculated. The value of ρ which produces the maximum net lifetime income then represents the choice of ρ by a government which selects that value preferred by a majority of the cohort.

8.2   THE DISTRIBUTION OF RATES OF RETURN

The internal rate of return to investment in higher education for an individual at the choice margin, y^*, is equal to the rate of interest, r. But the rate of return is higher for higher-income groups, so that it is not appropriate to refer to a single rate of return to education. The majority of studies of the effect of a change in the tax and transfer system on the incentive to invest in higher education unfortunately use a single measure of the rate of return, usually based on the age profile of average income. It should be stressed that this does not even correspond to an average rate of return. What is required to determine the effects of policy changes on the proportion educated is concentration on the rates of return around the educational choice margin.

The relationship between the private rate of return and the value of y can be found as follows. First, the total cost of higher education to the ith person is equal to the direct cost of education (net of the grant) plus the forgone earnings, and is given by:

$$y_i(1-t)(1-h)+c(1-\rho). \tag{8.12}$$

Secondly, the net benefit is measured by the difference between post-tax income in the second period, if investing, and post-tax income in the second period if not investing in higher education. This is equal to $y_i(1+s+g)$ $(1-t-t')-y_i(1+g)(1-t)$, which simplifies to:

$$y_i\{s(1-t-t')-t'(1+g)\}. \tag{8.13}$$

The rate of return to higher education for the ith individual is given by the discount rate, r_i, which equates the cost and the present value of net benefits, and is the solution to:

$$y_i(1-t)(1-h)+c(1-\rho)=y_i\{s(1-t-t')-t'(1+g)\}/(1+r_i). \quad (8.14)$$

This can be rearranged, where $\tilde{t}=t'/(1-t)$, to give:

$$r_i=\frac{uy_i(1-\tilde{t})-\tilde{t}(1+g)}{1-h+\dfrac{c(1-\rho)}{y_i(1-t)}}-1. \quad (8.15)$$

The variable $\tilde{t}$ can be interpreted as the surcharge expressed as a rate applied to the post-income-tax income calculated using the standard rate, t. Viewed this way, the surcharge is seen as paid out of post-tax income, so that the effective surcharge rate is higher than t'. Notice that $c(1-\rho)/y_i(1-t)$, which appears in the denominator of (8.15), is the ratio of the direct private cost of higher education net of the grant to net income in the first period, if working.

In using (8.15) to examine private rates of return it must be recognized that both t and g cannot be set exogenously, since they depend on the value of ρ and the other parameters of the model. An advantage of the present approach is that it considers these interdependencies explicitly. It is not appropriate to take the existing tax and grant structure as given, and simply impose a partial change in the tax structure such as a surcharge (equivalent to changing only t' in the expression for r_i). The introduction of a surcharge reduces the standard tax rate that would otherwise have to be charged, and changes the proportion investing in higher education (and consequently the external effects), along with the willingness of the non-educated majority to change the level of the grant. Further analysis of these interdependencies requires the use of numerical examples.

8.3   COMPARATIVE STATIC RESULTS

Individual Rates of Return

A tax surcharge of the type described above will leave the opportunity cost of higher education unaltered while raising the proportion of direct costs that individuals must repay in the form of deferred payments while working in the second period. It has been stressed above that even without a surcharge educated individuals make some deferred payment for their education by contributing higher taxes during their working lives. Thus the change in tax payments of educated individuals as a result of a surcharge is not given simply by the tax paid through the surcharge but requires consideration of the further effect of the surcharge on the standard tax rate which applies to all individuals. The precise orders of magnitude which may be relevant can only be investigated using numerical examples.

The choice of parameter values in this type of two-period model presents some awkward problems. The following calculations are based on the representative values of: $h = 0.2$; $u = 0.10$; $r = 0.60$; $\delta = 1.0$, $c = 5$ and $R = 6$. The value of r chosen may appear to be rather high, but in this type of two-period model many years are being compressed into the second period. However, the *comparisons* are not affected by the rate of interest used. For the distribution of y, the median value was as before set at 10 and the coefficient of variation at 0.5, giving a value of σ^2 of 0.233. Table 8.1 shows the value of the standard tax rate, t, needed to finance alternative combinations of ρ and t'. Table 8.1 shows that, for a given level of the grant, the standard tax rate, t, always falls as the tax surcharge rises. Thus for an individual investing in higher education, the rise in taxes paid through the surcharge is offset to some extent by the fall in the standard rate. It is impossible for the rise in taxes paid through the surcharge to be completely offset by a fall in the standard tax rate. However, the fall in the standard tax rate may affect individuals differently; and, in general, the possibility that a surcharge will favour some individuals more than others needs to be considered. Any study which neglected the implications of a surcharge for the standard tax rate would overestimate the effect of the surcharge on rates of return.

Table 8.1   *Standard tax rate for alternative surcharges*

	Tax surcharge, t'			
ρ	0	0.01	0.03	0.05
0	0.291	0.289	0.287	0.285
0.2	0.293	0.291	0.288	0.285
0.4	0.296	0.294	0.289	0.286
0.6	0.302	0.299	0.292	0.288
0.8	0.312	0.307	0.298	0.291
1.0	0.328	0.321	0.308	0.298

Comparisons of tax payments, for a given value of ρ, are shown in Table 8.2. This shows that the changes in the present value of total lifetime tax payments do not correspond to the amount of extra tax paid through the

Table 8.2   *Present values of tax payments*

$\rho = 0.75$

t'	85th percentile		95th percentile	
	Surcharge	Total tax	Surcharge	Total tax
0	0	9.868	0	15.428
0.03	0.852	10.237	1.356	16.050
0.05	1.411	10.544	2.249	16.560
Row 3 − Row 2	0.559	0.307	0.893	0.510

surcharge. Comparisons are given for two percentiles of the distribution of y. The measures shown in the last row of the table show that the extra amount paid through the surcharge when it increases from 0.03 to 0.05 overstates the extra lifetime tax contribution of the higher educated. For example, the total net lifetime tax of the 85th percentile increases by 0.307 units when the surcharge increases from 3 per cent to 5 per cent, but this is less than the increase directly attributable to the higher surcharge, of 0.559. These comparisons are all for a fixed value of ρ of 0.75. Notice that in each case the tax paid through the surcharge alone is much less than the value of the grant, which is $\rho c = 3.75$.

The increase in lifetime taxes suggests that rates of return to higher education will fall with the introduction of a surcharge, given a constant subsidy, or level of ρ. This is confirmed by the rates listed for a given ρ value, for alternative percentiles of the distribution of y given in Table 8.3. The final column also shows that the proportion educated falls with increases in the surcharge, which is not surprising given the fall in rates of return to higher education.

Table 8.3   *The effect of a surcharge on rates of return*

Rate of surcharge, t'	Rate of return for			Proportion investing, p
	75th percentile	85th percentile	95th percentile	
0	0.519	0.836	1.509	0.220
0.01	0.480	0.792	1.455	0.205
0.03	0.403	0.706	1.349	0.179
0.05	0.328	0.621	1.245	0.156

Induced Changes in the Grant

The results of the previous sub-section concern a situation in which the value of ρ, which determines the grant, is assumed to remain constant with the introduction of, or increase in, a tax surcharge. However, it would be expected that the level of the grant favoured by the majority of the population will be altered by the introduction of a tax surcharge. The level of grant favoured by the majority will change if either the marginal benefit or the marginal cost of providing a given grant for the majority of taxpayers is altered.

Marginal costs and benefits to the voter who does not invest in higher education can be considered explicitly as follows. The externality described above assumes that the general increase in earnings, g, is an increasing but marginally diminishing function of the proportion educated, p. Therefore, with a lower proportion educated as a result of a rise in t', the marginal benefit to the uneducated voters of increasing the grant will rise. The marginal cost of the grant to voters who do not invest in higher education consists of the increase in the tax they pay as a result of a rise in the standard tax rate needed to finance a higher grant. With a tax surcharge, a given increase in the grant implies that the increase in taxes paid by the uneducated voter will be lower than without the surcharge, since educated individuals pay a greater proportion of the costs of their own education in deferred income-contingent payments through the surcharge. Since marginal costs are lower and marginal benefits are higher, it would be expected that the introduction of a surcharge would lead uneducated voters to prefer a higher level of funding. This is confirmed in Table 8.4 where for the numerical simulation the grant preferred by the majority, ρ_m, is seen to increase as the tax surcharge is increased. This is shown in the second column of the table.

These induced changes in the grant should be considered as a general equilibrium consequence of the introduction of a tax surcharge, and estimates of the effect on rates of return to education must, at least where practicable, allow for this. The introduction of a tax surcharge which, *ceteris paribus*, reduces the rate of return to education for those above the choice margin, simultaneously induces an increase in ρ_m, which involves a compensating increase in the rate of return; thus the net effect on rates of return is unclear. Furthermore, rates of return can be expected to change differently for individuals with different values of y. Direct costs measured by c are constant for all educated individuals, so a rise in the subsidy will represent an equal absolute increase to all individuals. However, an increase in the surcharge affects high-income individuals relatively more. Thus rates of return for those with high y can be expected to rise by relatively less as ρ_m is increased.

Table 8.4 The effect of a surcharge on majority voting

t'	ρ_m	85th percentile		95th percentile		99th percentile		Average rate of return	Proportion educated
		Rate of return	Net lifetime income	Rate of return	Net lifetime income	Rate of return	Net lifetime income		
0	0.55	0.704	20.337	1.367	32.859	2.386	56.823	1.207	0.178
0.01	0.65	0.725	20.493	1.384	32.862	2.372	56.523	1.204	0.184
0.03	0.80	0.739	20.613	1.384	32.690	2.367	55.780	1.193	0.189
0.05	0.95	0.753	20.734	1.383	32.518	2.34	55.037	1.179	0.195

Changes in the Proportion Investing

Table 8.4 also shows the effects of the introduction of a surcharge on rates of return in this more general framework, for alternative percentiles of the distribution of y. The table shows that for nearly all educated members of the population, rates of return actually rise with the introduction of the surcharge, when the induced increase in the grant is considered. As expected, the rise in returns to higher education with the introduction of a surcharge is lower for those of high ability.

The arithmetic mean rate of return is shown in the penultimate column of Table 8.4, and is seen to fall as the surcharge increases. This shows that the average rate produces a misleading indication of the effect of the surcharge on the proportion of the population educated. The final two columns show that the fall in the average rate of return is accompanied by a rise in the proportion educated. This rise, which may at first seem paradoxical, comes about because rates of return are higher just above the choice margin, even though the very high-income members of the population are experiencing falling returns, which therefore reduces the average rate of return.

Although individual rates of return are a good indication of whether an individual will invest in education, they will not necessarily indicate whether they support changes in the financing of education. Referring to Table 8.4, it is shown that for very high-income individuals, those above the 99th percentile, a rise in the surcharge from 0 to 0.01 raises their rate of return when the induced increase in funding is taken into account. However, it also has the effect of lowering their net lifetime income. As these high-income individuals already invest in higher education, increases in the rate of return to this investment make it more profitable, but since higher education cannot be varied continuously in this framework, they are not able to increase this investment in response to the higher rate of return. On the cost side, the higher taxes the educated must pay with a surcharge lowers their net lifetime income by an amount which more than compensates for the increase in their rate of return. It is the effect on net lifetime income which ultimately determines whether an individual will support changes in the financing of higher education. In this situation the higher earners will not favour the introduction of the surcharge even accompanied by an increase in the grant, despite its leading to a higher rate of return.

Furthermore, rates of return may also be misleading indicators of an individual's support for higher education grants because of the externality generated by higher education. With an externality, it is possible that large rises in the surcharge may lower rates of return for a majority of educated individuals, despite the consequent increase in the level of the grant. These individuals may still support the changes, provided that the response of those previously below the choice margin, who are now induced to education, raises the external effect sufficiently to lead to an increase in the net lifetime income of those already educated.

8.4   A TAX SURCHARGE AND INEQUALITY

Instead of simply examining the implications for selected percentiles of the distribution of y, it is useful to examine the overall measures of inequality. Given the complexity of the model it is not possible to derive an explicit expression for any measure of inequality of net lifetime income. However, it is possible to calculate alternative measures by using a simulated cohort. Thus a 'population' of 15,000 individuals was produced by taking observations at random from the specified log normal distribution of income-earning ability, y. Having solved for the tax rate required, given the values of other parameters, and the educational choice margin, it is then simply necessary to take each 'random' individual, determine whether that person invests in higher education, and then calculate net lifetime income using either (8.1) or (8.2). Alternative inequality measures can then be calculated. Table 8.5 reports values of the coefficient of variation, η, the variance of logarithms, σ^2, and Atkinson's (1970) inequality measure, I(1.6), for an inequality aversion parameter of 1.6. These are all measures of the distribution of net lifetime income.

An increase in the level of the grant, with ρ_m unchanged, will induce an increase in inequality, since the grant is financed from general revenue but is paid only to those with high initial endowments. This is demonstrated by the first four rows of Table 8.5. This table also shows that for a given level of ρ, the level of inequality falls with the introduction of a tax surcharge, as seen in rows 5, 6 and 7. This is not surprising because, with a surcharge, more of the costs of education are borne by higher-income educated individuals.

Since the introduction of a surcharge raises the level of the grant favoured by a majority of the population, the net inequality implications of a surcharge depend on the relative magnitude of the direct fall in inequality, through the surcharge, compared with the rise in inequality through the induced increase in the level of the grant. The final three rows of Table 8.5 show that at the preferred ρ, all measures of inequality fall with the introduction of the surcharge, even though the level of the grant is raised. In these cases the direct effect of the surcharge on inequality outweighs the induced effect of the rise in the level of the grant.

This chapter has examined the interdependencies involved in the use of a higher education tax surcharge (which differs from a simple loan-repay-

Table 8.5   The effect of a surcharge on inequality

	η	σ^2	I(1.6)
$t'=0\begin{cases}\rho=0 \\ \rho=0.55 \\ \rho=0.8 \\ \rho=1.0\end{cases}$	0.688 0.707 0.714 0.718	0.270 0.286 0.296 0.305	0.203 0.214 0.220 0.226
$\rho=0.55\begin{cases}t'=0 \\ t'=0.03 \\ t'=0.05\end{cases}$	0.707 0.685 0.671	0.286 0.275 0.269	0.214 0.206 0.201
$t'=0,\quad\ \rho^*=0.55$ $t'=0.03,\ \ \rho^*=0.8$ $t'=0.05,\ \ \rho^*=0.95$	0.707 0.694 0.684	0.286 0.283 0.281	0.214 0.212 0.210

ment scheme). The willingness of those who do not invest in higher education to support the use of tax-financed grants is influenced not only by the extent of the external effects but by the progressivity of the tax system. A more progressive system shifts a large proportion of the costs of a grant towards the more highly educated in what are effectively deferred fees. But the disincentive effect of the taxes, in terms of the investment decision, must also be considered. A greater degree of progressivity is introduced by the existence of transfer payments in the form of a minimum income guarantee; this extra complication is examined in Appendix 8.1.

It was found that, for a fixed level of higher education grant, an increase in the tax surcharge is associated (through the government's budget constraint) with a reduction in the standard tax rate, along with a reduction in rates of return to investment in higher education and an associated reduction in the proportion of individuals investing. The increase in the surcharge is associated with a decrease in the dispersion of net lifetime income. These effects are a result of the extra degree of progression introduced into the tax system by the rise in the surcharge.

If, however, the size of the grant is (endogenously) determined within a public-choice framework, then a change in the surcharge will also affect the majority choice of the grant. When this endogenous change in voting behaviour is considered, an increase in the tax surcharge is found to be associated with an increase in the size of the grant. The arithmetic mean rate of return is found to fall, but this reduction arises from an *increase* in the rate of return for those near the educational choice margin, compensated by a fall in the rate of return for the very high-income earners (associated with

Table 8.6   A surcharge with a minimum-income guarantee

	85th percentile		95th percentile		99th percentile		Average		
	Rate of return	Net income	Rate of return	Net income	Rate of return	Net income	rate of return	Proportion educated	I(1.6)
$t' = 0, \rho_m = 0.6$	0.732	20.316	1.399	32.702	2.419	56.401	1.212	0.186	0.183
$t' = 0.3, \rho_m = 0.85$	0.771	20.593	1.417	32.534	2.401	55.357	1.191	0.200	0.180

Note: $m = 6.0$.

144

the increased progressivity of the tax system). The reduction in the rate of return for the high earners does not affect their investment decision (since the rate is well in excess of the market rate of interest), while the stimulus to investment provided by the higher rate of return at the margin leads to a rise in the proportion of the population investing. This shows the potentially misleading nature of a single summary measure of the distribution. Although an increase in the grant has, *ceteris paribus*, the effect of increasing inequality, the endogenous increase in the grant does not dominate the inequality-reducing effect of a higher surcharge. Hence a surcharge, combined with a grant increase, can both increase the proportion investing in higher education and reduce the inequality of net lifetime income. The model used is of course highly simplified, but it seems useful to consider the various interdependencies which are so often ignored in public debate.

APPENDIX 8.1   A SURCHARGE WITH A MINIMUM-INCOME GUARANTEE

A minimum-income guarantee can be introduced into the basic model, following the approach described in Chapter 7. Such a guarantee has no direct effect on the incentive facing individuals to invest in higher education, but of course there is an indirect influence through its impact on the government's budget constraint. The transfer system examined in this appendix is such that all those with a gross income below a specified level, m, have their net income brought up to the post-tax value of m. The following calculations use a value of m of 6.0, with other parameters the same as those. Table 8.6 shows the effects of the surcharge, combined with a minimum-income guarantee, on the rates of return and lifetime income for alternative percentiles of the population. It is seen from this table that the comparative static results are unaltered in comparison with the standard case. A surcharge leads to a higher level of the grant, lower marginal tax rates and a greater proportion educated. A slight difference of magnitude, however, is evident from the rates of return and lifetime income estimates; it is seen that the net lifetime income of individuals with high y declines more than in the standard case with increases in the tax surcharge. This suggests that average rates of return will be even more misleading as indicators of change in the proportion educated than in the standard case; this is supported by the relatively large increase in the proportion educated shown in the table. Finally, the inequality measure reinforces the distributive implications of the standard case.

References

Aitchison, J.A. and Brown, J.A.C. (1957) *The Lognormal Distribution*. Cambridge: Cambridge University Press.

Arcelus, F.J. and Levine, A.L. (1986) 'Merit goods and public choice: the case of higher education'. *Public Finance*, **41**, 303–14.

Atkinson, A.B. (1970) 'On the measurement of inequality'. *Journal of Economic Theory*, **2**, 244–63.

Atkinson, A.B. and Stiglitz, J. (1980) *Lectures on Public Economics*, New York, McGraw-Hill.

Bagehot, W. (1885) *The Postulates of English Political Economy*, with a preface by A. Marshall. London: Longmans, Green.

Barr, N. (1993) 'Alternative funding sources for higher education'. *Economic Journal*, **103**, 718–28.

Baum, S.R. and Schwartz, S. (1988) 'Merit goods and subsidies to college students'. *Economics of Education Review*, **7**, 127–34.

Becker, G.S. (1974) 'A theory of social interactions'. *Journal of Political Economy*, **82**, 1063–93.

Blaug, M. (1970) *An Introduction to the Economics of Education*. London: Penguin.

Blaug, M. (1989) 'Review of *Economics of Education: Research and Studies*'. *Journal of Human Resources*, **24**, 331–5.

Bös, D. (1980) 'The democratic decision on fees versus taxes'. *Kyklos*, **33**, 76–99.

Bowman, M.J. (ed.) (1986) *Collection Choice in Education*. Boston, Mass.: Kluwer-Nijhoff.

Brunner, J.K. (1986) 'A two-period model on optimal taxation with learning incentives'. *Journal of Economics/Zeitschrift fur Nationalökonomie*, **46**, 31–47.

Chapman, B.J. and Chia, T.-T. (1989) 'Financing higher education: private rates of return and externalities in the context of the tertiary tax'. ANU Centre for Economic Policy, *Research Discussion Paper 213*.

Chapman, A.B. and Harding, A. (1993) 'Australian student loans'. *Australian Economic Review*, 61–75.

Chinloy, M. (1980) 'Sources of quality change in labour input'. *American Economic Review*, **70**, 108–19.

Conlisk, J. (1977) 'A further look at the Hansen–Weisbrod–Pechman debate'. *Journal of Human Resources*, **12**, 147–63.

Crean, J.F. (1975) 'The income redistributive effect of public spending on higher education'. *Journal of Human Resources*, **10**, 116–22.

Creedy, J. (1985) *Dynamics of Income Distibution*. Oxford: Basil Blackwell.

Creedy, J. and Francois, P. (1990) 'Financing higher education and majority voting'. *Journal of Public Economics*, **24**, 181–200.

Creedy, J. and Francois, P. (1992a) 'Lifetime inequality and higher education grants: a public choice approach'. *Australian Economic Papers*, **31**, 146–57.

Creedy, J. and Francois, P. (1992b) 'Higher education and progressive taxation: equity, efficiency and majority voting'. *Journal of Economic Studies*, **19**, 17–30.

Creedy, J. and Francois, P. (1993a) 'Voting over income tax progression in a two-period model'. *Journal of Public Economics*, **50**, 291–8.

Creedy, J. and Francois, P. (1993b) 'Financing higher education: a general equilibrium public choice approach'. *Economic Record*, **69**, 1–9.

Creedy, J. and Francois, P. (1994) 'Financing higher education and a graduate tax surcharge'. *Labour Economics and Productivity*, 6, pp. 95–116.

Denison, E.F. (1984) 'Accounting for slower growth: an update'. In J. Kendrick (ed.), *International Comparisons of Productivity and Causes of the Slowdown*, Cambridge, Mass.: Ballinger.

De Wulf, L. (1981) 'Incidence of budgetary outlays: where do we go from here?' *Public Finance*, **36**, 56–76.

Green, J.R. and Sheshinski, E. (1975) 'A note on the progressivity of optimal public expenditure'. *Quarterly Journal of Economics*, **89**, 138–44.

Greene, K.V. (1973) 'Collective decision-making models and the measurement of benefits in fiscal incidence studies'. *National Tax Journal*, **26**, 177–85.

Hansen, W.L. and Weisbrod, B.A. (1969a) 'The distribution of costs and direct benefits of public higher education: the case of California'. *Journal of Human Resources*, **4**, 176–91.

Hansen, W.L. and Weisbrod, B.A. (1969b) *Benefits, Costs and the Finance of Public Higher Education*. Chicago: Markham.

Hare, P.G. (1988) 'Economics of publicly provided private goods and services'. In P.G. Hare (ed.), *Surveys in Public Sector Economics*, Oxford: Basil Blackwell, 68–101.

Hare, P.G. and Ulph, D.T. (1982) 'Imperfect capital markets and the public provision of education'. In M.J. Bowman (ed.), *Collective Choice in Education*. The Hague: Martinus Nijhoff, 103–30.

Haveman, R.H. and Wolfe, B.C. (1984) 'Schooling and economic well being: the role of non-market effects'. *Journal of Human Resources*, **19**, 377–407.

Holcombe, R.G. and Holcombe, L.P. (1984) 'The return to the federal government from investment in higher education'. *Public Finance Quarterly*, **12**, 365–72.

Hope, J. and Miller, P. (1988) 'Financing tertiary education: an examination of the issues'. *Australian Economic Review*, **4**, 37–57.

James, E. and Benjamin G. (1988a) 'Educational distribution and income redistribution through education in Japan'. *Journal of Human Resources*, **23**, 469–89.

James, E. and Benjamin, G. (1988b) *Public Policy and Private Education in Japan*. London: Macmillan.

Johnson, G.E. (1984) 'Subsidies for higher education'. *Journal of Labour Economics*, **2**, 303–18.

Jorgenson, D.W. (1984) 'The contribution of education to U.S. economic growth, 1948–1973'. In E. Dean (ed.), *Education and Economic Productivity*, Cambridge, Mass.: Ballinger.

Kendrick, J.W. (1983) *Inter-industry Differences in Productivity Growth*. Washington D.C.: American Enterprise Institute.

Lambert, P.J. (1993) *The Distribution and Redistribution of Income: A Mathematical Analysis*. Manchester: Manchester University Press.

Leslie, L.L. and Brinkman, P.T. (1988) *The Economic Value of Higher Education*. New York: Macmillan.

Lommerud, K.E. (1989) 'Education subsidies when relative incomes matter'. *Oxford Economic Papers*, **41**, 640–52.

Lovell, M.C. (1978) 'Spending for education: the exercise of public choice'. *Review of Economics and Statistics*, **60**, 487–95.

Majumdar, T. (1983) *Investment in Education and Social Choice*. Cambridge: Cambridge University Press.

McGuire, J.W. (1976) 'The distribution of subsidy to students in California public higher education'. *Journal of Human Resources*, **11**, 343–53.

McMahon, W.W. (1984) 'The relation of education and R&D to productivity growth'. *Economics of Education Review*, **3**, 299–313.

Pechman, J.A. (1970) 'The distributional effects of public higher education in California'. *Journal of Human Resources*, **5**, 230–6.

Psacharopoulos, G. (1973) *Returns to Education*. New York: American Elsevier.

Psacharopoulos, G. (1984) 'The contribution of education to economic growth'. In J.W. Kendrick (ed.), *International Comparisons of Productivity and Causes of the Slowdown*. Cambridge, Mass.: Ballinger.

Psacharopoulos, G. and Woodhall, M. (1985) *Education for Development: An Analysis of Investment Choices*. New York: Oxford University Press.

Roberts, K.W.S. (1977) 'Voting over income tax schedules'. *Journal of Public Economics*, **8**, 329–40.

Schultz, T.W. (1963) *The Economic Value of Education*. New York: Columbia University Press.

Schultz, T.W. (1981) *Investing in People*, Los Angeles, Cal.: University of California Press.

Shackett, J.R. and Slottje, D.J. (1987) 'Labour supply decisions, human capital attributes, and inequality in the size distribution of earnings in the U.S., 1952–81'. *Journal of Human Resources*, **22**, 82–100.

Smyth, D.J. (1991) 'A model of quality changes in higher education'. *Journal of Economic Behaviour and Organisation*, **15**, 151–7.

Ulph, D. (1977) 'On the optimal distribution of income and education expenditure'. *Journal of Public Economics*, **8**, 351–6.

Index